As one of the world's longe
and best-known
Thomas Cook are the ex

For more than 135 y
guidebooks have unlocked the secrets
of destinations around the world,
sharing with travellers a wealth of
experience and a passion for travel.

**Rely on Thomas Cook as your
travelling companion on your next trip
and benefit from our unique heritage.**

Thomas Cook **traveller** guides

ALGARVE & SOUTHERN PORTUGAL

**Susie Boulton, Joe Staines,
Sarah Le Tellier, Martin Symington**

Your travelling companion since 1873

Written by Susie Boulton, Joe Staines, Sarah Le Tellier and
Martin Symington, updated by Barbara Rogers

Published by Thomas Cook Publishing
A division of Thomas Cook Tour Operations Limited
Company registration no. 3772199 England
The Thomas Cook Business Park, Unit 9, Coningsby Road,
Peterborough PE3 8SB, United Kingdom
Email: books@thomascook.com, Tel: + 44 (0) 1733 416477
www.thomascookpublishing.com

Produced by Cambridge Publishing Management Limited
Burr Elm Court, Main Street, Caldecote CB23 7NU
www.cambridgepm.co.uk

ISBN: 978-1-84848-363-7

2003, 2007, 2009 Thomas Cook Publishing
This fourth edition © 2011
Text © Thomas Cook Publishing
Maps © Thomas Cook Publishing/PCGraphics (UK) Limited

Series Editor: Karen Beaulah
Production/DTP: Steven Collins

Printed and bound in Spain by GraphyCems

Cover photography © Marco Simoni/Superstock

Contents

Introduction

Portugal is the westernmost country of mainland Europe, with over 800km (497 miles) of coastline facing the vast expanse of the Atlantic Ocean. The sea has dominated Portugal's history, from the great voyages of discovery in the late 15th century to the fleets of fishermen who still journey as far as Newfoundland and Greenland in search of their catch.

For such a small country, Portugal is remarkably varied, and there is a notable difference between the north and the south. The character of southern Portugal has been influenced by its proximity to Africa, and by successive visitors from the Mediterranean – Phoenicians, Romans and Moors – who have all left their distinctive imprint. In particular, the Moorish occupation of the south, which began in AD 711 and continued until 1249, had a lasting effect on the region's architecture, crafts, agriculture and arts.

Today, visitors from all over the world flock to the thin strip of Portugal's southern coast that makes up the Algarve. Even with the transforming effect of recent tourism development, this region retains its appeal. It enjoys an equable climate, with hardly any summer rain, and long stretches of perfect sandy beach, not to mention good, simple food and a warm and welcoming people. For those for whom beach life is not an attraction, there is much else to discover in the south. The huge plain of the Alentejo remains underexplored by visitors; like the Algarve, it erupts into a colourful riot of wild flowers between February and June. It also possesses a wealth of historical monuments and works of art, many of them concentrated in the exquisite and ancient city of Évora. Finally, for those fed up with the bustle of modern life, the isolated villages along the Spanish border provide the perfect escape.

'Where the land ends and the sea begins…
LUÍS DE CAMÕES, from *The Lusiads*, 1572

'In the sea off Lusitania acorn-bearing oaks grow, upon which the tunnies feed and fatten themselves…'
POLYBIUS, from the *Histories*, c.150 BC

'Everywhere the children regard us with a savage confidence. Here [Lagos] they are quite troublesome in impudence. How do

the Portuguese live…? Fish and pulse and bread!! Mutton they dislike even when good. At Faro it is often called goat's flesh to make it saleable.'
ROBERT SOUTHEY, from his *Portuguese Journal,* 1800–1

'It was evening; herds of black goats, driven by little boys and girls in great straw hats, tripped along the dusty road; small donkeys ambled home, their panniers full of water pots or vegetables or turf; the smell of flowers and sticky fig leaves drifted on the warm air.'
ROSE MACAULAY on the Algarve, from *Fabled Shore,* 1949

'I passed the day succeeding my arrival principally in examining the town [Évora] and its environs, and as I strolled about, entered into conversation with various people that I met; several of these were of the middle class… When I spoke of religion, they exhibited the utmost apathy for the subject, and making their bows, left me as soon as possible.'
GEORGE BORROW, from *The Bible in Spain,* 1843

'The fields in these days of mid-June had the first golden ears of ripe corn, waving and fat, which the breeze bends down in groups of gracious welcome. On both sides, between sheaves piled up anyhow, the scarlet of the poppies was laughing like the lips of ardent girls.'
JOSÉ FIALHO DE ALMEIDA on the Alentejo, from *Aves Migradoras,* 1893

Brightly painted fishing boats are a characteristic feature of the Algarve

The region

Portugal, occupying the western strip of the Iberian peninsula, looks small and modest on the map, especially when compared with its neighbour, Spain. Indeed, Portugal's land area (91,951sq km/35,500sq miles) takes up less than one-fifth of the peninsula and yet it still manages to be a country of astonishing diversity, both in its physical characteristics and in its differing ways of life.

Portugal is bounded to the north and the east by Spain and to the south and the west by the Atlantic Ocean. It is a continuation of the Iberian Meseta, or high tableland, which slopes gradually down to the sea in the south. The highest mountain range is the Serra da Estrela, in the middle of the country, which rises to 2,000m (6,562ft). The climate is extremely temperate, with most of the low rainfall occurring in winter and more heavily in the north than in the south.

The Algarve

The Algarve is the southernmost region of Portugal. It is separated from Spain, to the east, by the Guadiana River and from the Alentejo region, to the north, by two mountain ranges, the Serra de Monchique and the Serra do Caldeirão. These mountains, which cover almost two-thirds of the region, are made up of carboniferous shale that disintegrates easily and cultivation is practically impossible due to erosion. Apart from the spa of Caldas de Monchique, this mountainous area is therefore rarely visited. Immediately to the south of the mountains is a limestone zone that runs across the region from east to west, known as the Barrocal, a name that suggests wasteland as much as limestone. In fact, much of the Barrocal is cultivated; almonds, figs, olives and carob grow here in abundance and are an important part of the Algarvian economy.

Of course, most visitors to the Algarve come for the coast, the western half of which, from Cabo de São Vicente (Cape St Vincent) to Faro, is famous for its golden cliffs, full of caves and crevices, and its small sheltered beaches. The eastern half, called the Sotavento and stretching from Faro to Vila Real de Santo António, has a less dramatic, but equally sun-drenched, succession of sandy beaches. Tourism now vies with fishing as the major industry of the area, but the centuries-old pursuit of the sardine and the tuna still thrives.

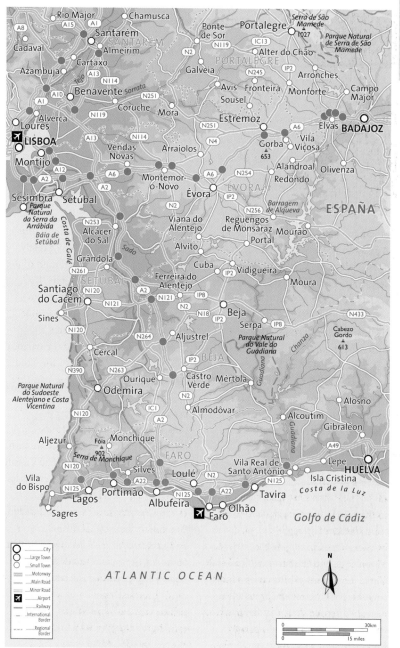

City
Large Town
Small Town
Motorway
Main Road
Minor Road
Airport
Railway
International Border
Regional Border

The Alentejo

This region, north of the Algarve, consists of one vast and level plain, except for the mountains of the Serra de Marvão and the Serra de São Mamede in the northeast. Most of the land is divided into large estates, or *latifundios*, centred around a farm complex called a *monte*. The region has no really big towns or cities. Évora and Beja both have relatively small populations.

Arable farming predominates, but there is also much unfarmed heathland as well as extensive cork oak forests; processing of the bark is an important industry, both here and in the Algarve. Traditional, but increasingly uncommon, are the great flocks of sheep. The region is known for its *porco preto* – black pig – an Iberian breed whose meat is favoured by chefs. Look for them especially around Borba and Estremoz.

Centuries of exploitation by (often absentee) landlords have made the Alentejanos the most politically radical and anti-clerical of all the Portuguese. The Alentejo has been consistent in its support of the Communist Party. Despite the land reforms that followed the Carnation Revolution of 1974, this is still an economically depressed region with a high level of unemployment. It is famed, however, for being meticulously clean and tidy, and the villagers of the region take pride in their simple lime-washed houses, which they decorate with borders of ochre or pale grey.

Flora

Portugal might be on the Atlantic coast, but the south, at least, has more of a Mediterranean climate, with the result that the area has a particularly rich flora and a magnificent array of literally thousands of species of wild flowers that cram themselves into every nook and cranny, clinging precariously to dunes and rocky cliff faces. From February to June, the entire landscape turns into a blaze of colour as the plants rush to flower. By the start of the main tourist season, in July and August, the land is once again parched and brown.

Coastal plants

Of all the coastal plants, perhaps the most common is the *cistus*, or rock rose, found here in a dozen different forms.

On the beaches, other common plants include sea-heath and matted sea knotgrass, bushy sea spurge and sea stocks, thrift (*Armeria pungens*), which has tall pink flowers, and cream-flowered milk vetch (*Astragalus massiliensis*), nicknamed the 'hedgehog plant' because of its rounded, spiky clumps. Above all, keep an eye out for the bizarre, parasitic saltmarsh broomrape (*Cistanche phelypea*), which pokes out of the bare sand like a yellow-flowered asparagus stalk.

Fields, hills and woodlands

Although much of the Alentejo consists of rolling prairie, given over largely to

A carpet of poppies and marigolds

wheat production, it is as yet virtually untouched by herbicides, and hundreds of species of native field flowers still thrive. The cultivated trees, such as almond, olive, fig, orange and lemon, are themselves a wonderful sight in full flower, but they also provide shelter for a host of shade-loving wild flowers.

In the volcanic mountains that separate the Algarve from the Alentejo, the vegetation is lusher and greener. Rhododendrons run wild beside the road, along with the extraordinary strawberry tree, while behind are thick groves of beech, chestnut, birch, maple and several different species of oak. Predominant among these are the evergreen, tauzin and the cork oak, an indigenous tree, left to its own devices except at harvest time.

The Maquis

As you head inland, you find yourself wrapped in the heady fragrance of the Mediterranean-style scrubland that covers many of the infertile hills. Herbs grow in the shade provided by conifers, while wild irises, squills, tassel hyacinths and catchfly (*Silene colorata*) add patches of bright colour. Hunt carefully among the rocks and you can find several different species of the shy bee orchid (*Ophrys*) family. The thorny Judas tree, the luxuriant oleander and the carob (*Ceratonia siliqua*) are all old indigenous species that somehow managed to avoid destruction during successive Ice Ages. Known by the Arabs as *kirat*, it was the weight of the carob bean that set the carat standard used ever since as a measure for diamonds and other precious stones. Today, it is harvested commercially for use as a gum for papermaking, as a food stabiliser, as cattle feed and, for humans, as a slightly healthier alternative for chocolate.

History

Around 2000 BC	Iberian tribes arrive in the peninsula.
Around 1000 BC	Phoenicians set up trading stations and settlements in the Algarve.
Around 700 BC	Invasion of Celtic settlers, who become Celtiberians.
Around 210 BC	Occupation by the Romans. The Algarve area, along with northwest Africa, is named Cyneticum.
Around 27 BC	The province south of the Douro River is named Lusitania.
Around AD **200**	Introduction of Christianity.
Around 409	The peninsula is invaded by central European tribes.
415	Visigoths invade Iberia.
711	Moors conquer the peninsula. The areas now known as the Algarve and the Alentejo are named al-Gharb al-Andalus ('the west of Andalus') and occupied mainly by Yemenites.
1086	The peninsula is invaded by the Almoravides of North Africa against the Christian reconquest.
1139	Afonso Henriques defeats a Muslim army in the Alentejo and declares himself King of Portugal.
1147	Lisbon is recaptured from the Muslims.
1189	King Sancho I of Portugal captures Silves, the Moorish capital of the Algarve.
1249	King Afonso III of Portugal completes the reconquest of the Algarve, ending Moorish rule.
1385	A Castilian army invades Portugal but is defeated. The victorious leader of the Portuguese army is crowned King João I and establishes a matrimonial alliance with England.
1415	Portuguese imperial expansion begins in Morocco.
1418	Prince Henry 'the Navigator' (son of King

João I) becomes governor of the Algarve.

1498 Vasco da Gama sails to India.

1578 The Portuguese army is annihilated by the Moroccans at the battle of Alcácer-Quibir.

1580 King Philip II of Spain unites Portugal and Spain.

1587 Sir Francis Drake attacks Lagos and Sagres, destroying the house and navigational school of Henry the Navigator.

1640 The Duke of Bragança restores Portuguese independence.

1755 An earthquake destroys Lisbon and much of the Algarve and the Alentejo.

1807 Napoleon's army invades Portugal; the royal family flees to Brazil.

1808–11 The Peninsular War. British and Portuguese troops under Wellington drive the French out of Portugal.

1908 Republican activists assassinate King Carlos I.

1910 Republican Revolution. King Manuel II is forced to abdicate.

1933 After 23 years of turmoil and economic decline, Prime Minister Salazar establishes the totalitarian 'New State'.

1974 The 'Carnation Revolution'. A new democratic constitution is drawn up and elections lead to victory for the Socialist-led government of Prime Minister Soares.

1975 Mozambique, Angola and East Timor are given their independence.

1986 Portugal joins the EU. Soares is the first civilian president of Portugal.

2010 The Alentejo wins the Tourism Oscar for Portugal's best national tourist region, a prize normally won by the Algarve.

2011 Presidential elections. The world's largest solar photovoltaic farm becomes fully operational near Moura, capable of generating 93GWh of electricity annually.

Politics

Portugal ceased to be a monarchy in 1910 after the bloodless Republican Revolution forced the last king, Manuel II, into exile in Britain. The Republican Party's main target, after the monarchy, was the power of the Catholic Church, which it effectively outlawed. Universal male suffrage was introduced in 1911 and a new constitution drawn up.

However, divisions within the party rapidly developed, the much-needed land reforms failed to materialise, and stable government seemed an impossibility. In 1926, after 45 governments in 16 years, a military coup took place. Under President Carmona, parliament was suspended, strikes were banned and censorship was introduced. Then, in 1928, António Salazar, Professor of Economics at Coimbra University, was appointed Minister of Finance.

The New State

Salazar's main task was to remedy the country's disastrous economic situation, caused by a substantial national debt. This he more or less achieved by pursuing an extreme monetarist policy, virtually cutting all public spending. In 1930, he founded the National Union Party and two years later he became prime minister, a position he held until he suffered a stroke, causing his retirement, in 1968.

The Estado Novo or 'New State' that he presided over was a right-wing dictatorship modelled on Italian Fascism. It was less overtly militaristic and expansionist than other fascist regimes, but no less brutal in the suppression of its opponents through its secret police force, the PIDE. Strikes and trade unions were banned, only one political party was permitted and suffrage was limited. At the same time, the modernisation of the country's industry and infrastructure remained slow and half-hearted, with Portugal remaining dependent on its colonies for many commodities and raw materials.

The Carnation Revolution

Despite the moderate reforms of Salazar's successor, Caetano, increasing dissatisfaction with the colonial wars in Africa led a group of radical army officers to organise a revolution. On 25 April 1974, the Armed Forces Movement (MFA), supported by Communist and Socialist parties, took control of Lisbon. Spontaneous popular support followed, with demonstrators placing red carnations in the soldiers' guns. A Revolutionary Council was set up, following an attempted military counter-coup, and a year later the first free elections since 1926 were held.

The Socialist Party (PS) won 38 per cent of the vote and the Popular Democrats (PPD) were next with 26 per cent. A coalition government introduced a programme of decolonisation, nationalisation and land reform, turning the vast estates of the south into workers' cooperatives. A Socialist constitution, introduced in 1976, established Portugal as a republican, parliamentary democracy, but over the next ten years, the failure by any party to win an overall majority led to uneasy alliances and increasing economic instability.

Recent developments

After more than a decade of coalition governments, the right-of-centre Social Democratic Party (PSD) won a clear parliamentary majority in 1987. Their leader, Aníbal Cavaco Silva, was elected president, serving until 2011, although the Socialists won a majority in 2005 and again in 2009, led by Prime Minister José Sócrates. The 2009 elections were won by a narrower margin, but the Socialists have managed to continue their progressive policies through alliances with the left on social issues, such as same-sex marriage, and the right for fiscal reforms necessary to combat the growing budget deficit that exceeds the 3 per cent limit allowed by the eurozone. Portugal has until 2013 to bring that deficit into line, the same year as the next parliamentary elections.

Politics

Faro's pretty main square

Culture

Southern Portugal – south of the Tejo (Tagus) River – looks and feels utterly different from the north. This is largely due to the legacy of the Moors, whose presence in the region lasted over five centuries. Monuments to their culture are fewer and less spectacular than in neighbouring Andalucía; they include the castle at Silves, parts of a mosque at Mértola and the remains of the Moorish quarter at Moura.

The domestic architecture of the Algarve and the Alentejo has, however, a distinctively North African character – not just in the squareness of the buildings and their whitewashed exteriors, but also in the ornate filigree chimneys of the Algarve and the distinctive roof terraces of Olhão, and everywhere are the decorated glazed tiles called *azulejos*. The Moors also left their mark on the land with the introduction of rice, figs and, of course, the almond, which blossoms so gloriously in February.

Manueline architecture

Southern Portugal is not known primarily for the quality of its church architecture, but for one short period, in the late 15th and 16th centuries, there came a burst of building activity that created a new and unique style.

Elsewhere in Europe, High Gothic art reached its pinnacle as the Renaissance swung into action in Italy. The Portuguese were hot on the trail of new colonies and trade routes; and in Spain, Ferdinand and Isabel (the 'Catholic Monarchs') flung the last of the Moors off the Iberian peninsula, along with 250,000 Jews, topping off their actions by letting loose the Inquisition.

Their influence spread across the border, and this became the great age of Christian fervour. As town after town rushed to build ever more glorious churches, Manueline architecture was born, named after King Manuel I, who reigned from 1490 to 1520.

In shape, the church remained basically Gothic, but ceilings became even higher and the arches widened. Above all, the decorative themes changed, becoming more lavish and less overtly religious. With the whole country peering over the horizon, nautical motifs became increasingly prominent – with twisted columns rising to corded arches and stars, globes, knots and anchors appearing on bosses and portals – while doors and windows were often garlanded with laurel leaves, roses, poppies and even artichokes.

Arts and crafts

Since the advent of tourism many traditional crafts, previously on the verge of extinction, have been revived and there is a wealth of *artesanato* shops and stalls to choose from. Much of the art and crafts on sale is genuine local fare, but there is also much that is mass-produced, masquerading as handicraft, especially in the Algarve.

The Alentejo

Arraiolos, to the north of Évora, is famed for its carpets. The designs consist of formalised flowers or animals, made up with an unusual cross stitch; natural dyes are used, which mellow with age. In Estremoz,

naive ceramic figurines (*bonecos de Estremoz*) are made, often of saints or historical characters. The museum there contains a workshop that makes reproductions of originals, and has typical Alentejan rooms with hand-painted furniture.

Unaccompanied male-voice choirs are another of the region's notable and thriving artistic traditions. Their songs tell of the physical hardship endured while working the land, in melancholy but stirring three- or four-part harmony.

The Algarve

Though neither region has a particular local costume, the women in the mountains of the Algarve wear large black woollen shawls. Weaving is widespread; rugs, shawls, bedspreads and donkey saddlebags are available, most plentifully in Silves. Lacework and crocheting were once common handicrafts, and the women of Azinhal were famous for the delicacy of their lace, but the skill has now almost entirely died out. Basketry has not disappeared and a variety of types are made throughout the region. The village of Odeleite, near the Guadiana River, is still a centre for baskets made of split cane. Baskets can also be found at Loulé, though this town is better known for its coppersmiths; they make a wide range of pots and pans, including the *cataplana*, a pan made of two halves that are clipped together when cooking.

A blend of Moorish and classical architecture in Aljustrel

Azulejos

The *azulejo*, or glazed tile, is one of the most characteristic features of Portuguese decorative art. At one time only wealthy Portuguese could afford to live in a house decorated with tiles. Nowadays the *azulejo* is completely classless, decorating the façades of even the simplest dwellings and outbuildings.

It was the Moorish influence that led to the Portuguese passion for *azulejos*. Nobody agrees about the origin of the word, but it may be derived from the Arabic *al Zulaicha* or *Zuleija*, meaning ceramic mosaic, or simply from the Portuguese word *azul*, meaning blue.

Tiles really came into vogue during the period from 1580 to 1640 when Portugal was under Spanish rule. The earliest tiles were imported from Andalucía, but soon the Portuguese

Azulejos have withstood the vagaries of the climate and are freely used as surface decoration on buildings …

... and to decorate street signs and furniture

started to develop their own. The second half of the 17th century saw the arrival of the narrative tiles. Churches were subsequently decorated with biblical scenes, and private palaces with fables, hunting scenes or depictions of everyday life.

By the middle of the 18th century, tiled scenes had become lavish and were typified by floral designs, cherubs and hedonistic scenes, influenced by rococo painters. However, the rebuilding of Portugal after the catastrophic earthquake of 1755 led to the mass production of *azulejos* in simpler styles. Fortunately, some of the small

family businesses, using traditional tilemaking techniques, managed to survive.

In the Algarve, the church of São Lourenço, Almancil (*see p66*), stands out for its gloriously tiled interior. Also worth seeing are the antique tiled panels in the gardens at Estói (*see p69*) and the tiled scenes from the life of St Francis in the church of São Francisco in Faro (*see p58*).

In the Alentejo, the finest examples can be found in the cloister and chapterhouse of the convent of Nossa Senhora da Conceição in Beja (*see pp86–7*) and in the church of the Convento dos Lóios in Évora (*see p102*).

Festivals

Scarcely a week goes by without some town or village in Portugal honouring a local saint or celebrating a local custom. Fairs, festivals and folk pilgrimages are all events worth catching, and the smaller the village the more jolly and intimate the occasion tends to be. Some of the dates of these festivities vary from year to year so it is worth checking with the tourist office before heading off into the back of beyond.

January

Between New Year's Day and Epiphany small groups perform New Year 'carols' in the streets.

February

The small Alentejan town of Mourão celebrates the **Feast of the Purification of the Virgin** with a festive procession on the second day of the month. Lent begins on Ash Wednesday, in late February or early March, and the preceding days are filled with Carnaval festivities throughout Portugal. The region's best are in Loulé, where the highlights are a parade of elaborate floats and the Battle of Flowers.

There is also an international cross-country race held at a different location in the Algarve each year.

March/April

The **Mass of the Easter Vigil**, celebrated late on the Saturday evening preceding Easter Sunday, often includes a grand procession with a band and floats, and sometimes flowers are strewn in the streets.

In Loulé, at Easter, there is a unique *romaria* (pilgrimage) celebrating the Sovereign Mother (Mãe Soberana).

On 25 April, there is a national holiday to commemorate the 1974 Revolution that ended the dictatorship.

May

May Day is a national holiday; many towns and villages celebrate with folk festivals, of which the most picturesque is held in the Algarvian village of Alte. For the first three days of May the town of Estói has its own **Festival of the Pine** (Festa da Pinha), whereas the town of Vila Viçosa celebrates the last two days with a country fair. Salir celebrates the **Grain Festival** (Festa da Espiga) in the second week of the month.

May/June/July

The **Algarve Music Festival**: concerts, recitals and ballet performances across the province.

June

A national holiday, on 10 June, celebrates the poet Camões and Portuguese communities scattered throughout the world. On 13 June, the **Feast of St Antony** (Festa de Santo António), the Lisbon-born saint, is celebrated in many southern towns, especially in Reguengos in the Alentejo.

The **Feast of St John the Baptist** (São João), another popular saint, is celebrated in various parts of the region on 23, 24 and 25 June. One of the biggest festivals is held in Évora over three days starting on 24 June.

July

Around 16 July the **Festival of Nossa Senhora do Carmo** is held in Faro to celebrate the Virgin's protection of fishermen. Silves is the setting for a beer festival held in the third week of the month and involves music-making as well as drinking. From 18 to 26 July the tiny medieval town of Monsaraz stages a festival of music and handicrafts.

August

The small port of Olhão celebrates the plenitude of sardines and other fish by staging a seafood festival. In Castro Marim, on the Guadiana River, they celebrate the **Feast of Our Lady of Martyrs** between 15 and 17 August with a festival and a fair. In the Alentejo, there are festivities at Castelo de Vide on 10 August and at Beja between 10 and 15 August.

September

This is the month of the **Algarve Folk Music and Dance Festival**, held across the province, which usually peaks in the middle of the month. The harvest season prompts a big livestock fair in Moura early in September and major market fairs in Elvas mid-month and Viana do Alentejo at the end of September.

October

A national holiday commemorating the founding of the Republic in 1910 occurs on 5 October.

Faro stages another festival around 20 October in celebration of Santa Iria. In the mountain town of Monchique there is a big country fair between 26 and 28 October, and an impressively large one is held in the small Alentejan town of Castro Verde on 18 October.

November

All Saints' Day on 1 November is a national holiday, and **All Souls' Day** on 2 November is an important religious feast.

December

The first day of the month is the anniversary of the day in 1640 when the Portuguese restored one of their own monarchs to the throne after 60 years of Spanish rule. **Christmas Day** is celebrated as a religious feast in a restrained fashion.

Impressions

The Portuguese are not as outgoing as the Spanish, and this is especially true of the Alentejans, but on the whole they are extremely friendly and polite. In remoter areas, staring at strangers is a sign of curiosity and is not meant aggressively. People are very helpful when their assistance is sought. In those parts of the Algarve most transformed by tourism, a certain brusqueness is not uncommon.

What to find and where

Beaches

The beaches of the Algarve, in spite of mass tourism, remain some of the most beautiful in Europe. Unfortunately, the best, including the famous Praia da Rocha, are often the most over-developed. Remember that there will be less crowding the further you move away from the main beach of any resort. Fishing boats and small ferries offer an attractive alternative, taking passengers to secluded cove beaches that have no access from the cliffs above, or to some of the small islands just offshore in the Ria Formosa. For comparative emptiness, try the Alentejan coast, especially between Vila Nova de Milfontes and Zambujeiro do Mar.

Castles

Some of Portugal's finest castles lie in the south, and their histories include Moors, Knights Templar and an uneasy relationship with Spain. Silves is crowned by Portugal's finest Moorish fortification. The prize in the Alentejo must go to Beja or the well-preserved castellated town of Moncão, but Castelo de Vide and Serpa are contenders.

Flowers

Spring comes early in the south, and from February through to June there is an explosion of many-coloured blossoms in the Algarve and the Alentejo. The pink and white almond blossom in February is particularly spectacular and by April most of the region's wild flowers are blooming. It has been estimated that the native flora consists of over 1,200 species.

Monuments

Concentrations of prehistoric remains, including dolmens, menhirs and stone circles, are found in the Alentejo, west of Évora and around the medieval hill town of Monsaraz. Not so well known as those in the Alentejo is the dense cluster of prehistoric sites east of Sagres. The Alentejo has more to offer architecturally than the Algarve, especially at Évora, where there is a Roman temple and a medieval cathedral. The excavated Roman villa of Milreu, at Estói, includes the remains of a 4th-century chapel.

Mountains

The Serra de Monchique is the most fertile and accessible of the Algarvian mountains, and a visit to the spa of Caldas de Monchique and the town of Monchique makes a good contrast to the bustle of the beach.

In the Serra de São Mamede, in the Alto Alentejo, the fortress towns of Portalegre, Marvão and Castelo de Vide provide wonderful views into Spain and, on clear days, as far as the Serra da Estrela in the north.

Sport

The Algarve has an increasing number of sports facilities. Golf has proved to be very popular, with demand out-numbering courses, despite the expense. The Quinta do Lago and Penina courses are the best and most exclusive in Portugal.

Facilities for watersports, such as windsurfing, waterskiing, sailing and diving, are available all along the Algarve coast and in the Alentejo at Vila Nova de Milfontes. Recently, facilities have sprung up at some of the inland reservoirs. There is a large marina at Vilamoura where yachts and motor-boats can be hired.

Impressions

The curiously shaped rocks and bays of the Praia do Camilo

Fishermen still tend their nets along the beach

The people
Dress

Though more relaxed in the south, attitudes to dress are quite conservative. Professional people always dress well. For men this means that jacket and tie are *de rigueur*, an attitude that applies to foreigners only in some first-class hotels. Women should not expose too much flesh when visiting churches.

Driving

Portugal has one of the worst records for accidents in Europe. Part of it may be due to the many narrow and precipitous mountain roads, especially in the north, but foolhardy overtaking on motorways certainly contributes. That said, the Portuguese tend to be courteous drivers.

Football

Football is a national obsession; the national side is one of Europe's stronger teams. There is a daily newspaper, *Bola*, given over entirely to football news. Attending a game is an easy-going, family affair, though none of the top clubs comes from the south.

Greetings

It is standard for men to greet each other with a handshake. Women greeting male or female friends usually do so with a kiss on both cheeks, a custom not extended to strangers.

Language

The Portuguese language is not difficult to learn but its nasal sounds are difficult to pronounce and even more so to understand (*see* Practical guide, *pp184–5*). Making an attempt to speak even a few phrases will be appreciated, but many Portuguese speak good English.

Lifestyle

The Portuguese enjoy a siesta period in the afternoon to avoid the midday heat. Family evening strolls around town are also a popular pastime.

Manners

People expect to be treated with respect and courtesy. It is regarded as impolite to stretch or yawn in public.

Patriotism

The Portuguese are intensely proud of the achievements of their country during its long history. It is not a good idea to be critical unless speaking to someone you know well. There is a certain mild animosity towards the Spanish.

Religion

The majority of the population is Roman Catholic but religious observance is much less strict in the south than in the north of Portugal.

Smoking and spitting

In January 2008, new legislation banned smoking in almost all public places. The only exceptions are bars and restaurants over 100sq m (1,076sq ft),

which are allowed a specifically designated smoking area. Among men, noisy spitting in the street is extremely commonplace.

Women

There are no particular problems for women travelling alone in Portugal, although as anywhere it is strongly advisable not to hitchhike. However, visitors should note that Portuguese society is not as liberal as that of some European countries and women may give the wrong impression by drawing attention to themselves especially with scanty clothing.

Impressions

Boats in the marina at Lagos

Western Algarve

Most of the photographs showing the Algarve as a land of golden sand beaches caught in coves beneath soaring, wildly carved rock cliffs were taken in this stretch of coast between Albufeira and Cabo de São Vicente, each landscape more dramatic than the last, with the soft stone eroded into fantastic shapes by the Atlantic waves and winds.

Between these headlands and along the bays that carve the western end of the coast are long sand beaches at Luz and Salema, one end of the latter shared with fishermen. More long strands account for the popularity of the coast around Albufeira.

So beautiful is this quintessential Algarve that it also shares the other stereotype of Portugal's playground in the sun: overdeveloped and overcrowded. Don't look here for the sleepy fishing villages of yore – those fishermen's cottages are now dressed up as quaint tourist lodgings, and an unfortunate number of those glorious eroded cliffs are topped by layers of high-rise buildings and hotels.

That's not to suggest that the Algarve does not have a thriving local life of its own. It does, and the fishermen still go out each day to catch all those sardines that grill so invitingly at lunchtime. But the conversations in the street – and certainly on the beach – will be a happy mix of many languages, and the colourful fishing boats do double duty ferrying beachgoers to those secret coves.

It's a happy blend that locals have adjusted to with the good humour that comes with an improved economy. And only a short distance inland, north of the east–west road SS 125, is a completely different Algarve, landscapes of olive, citrus and almond groves that rise quickly into the Serra de Monchique. Here it's possible to feel the old Algarve, a place of sleepy little whitewashed villages and the attractive town of Silves, under its Moorish castle.

Lagos

For two centuries, the harbour town of Lagos was the capital of the Algarve. Henry the Navigator had his headquarters here and it was to Lagos that ocean-going caravels returned, laden with sugar, grain and gold from Africa and the East Indies. In 1434, the explorer Gil Eanes left Lagos on his pioneering voyage round Cape Bojador, farther than any European had ventured before.

Western Algarve

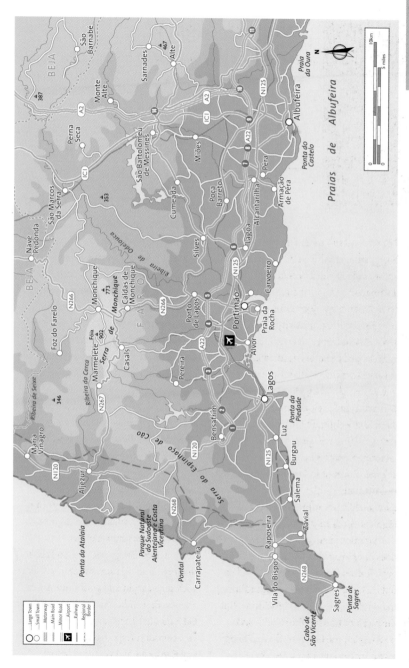

It was also from here, in 1578, that the fanatical King Sebastião set sail on his North African crusade, which culminated in the disastrous battle at Alcácer-Quibir, when almost his entire army was destroyed, and with it the flower of the Portuguese aristocracy.

Today, Lagos serves as a centre for northern European holidaymakers staying in the coastal resorts of the western end of the Algarve. Despite devastation by the 1755 earthquake, and more recently by the tidal wave of tourism, the town still has a certain elegance.

The **fort** and part of the city walls still stand, its narrow streets are stone paved and some fine old churches remain. This plus its abundance of cafés, restaurants and small shops makes Lagos one of the coast's favourite towns.

Most of the town's sights are within a short distance of the Praça da República (confusingly also called the Praça Infante Dom Henrique) where a large bronze statue of Henry the Navigator, sextant in hand, looks out to sea.

Fort: Antigos Paços do Concelho, Praça Gil Eanes. Tel: 282 764111. www.cm-lagos.pt. Open: Mon–Fri 9.30am–6.30pm, Sat & Sun 9am–1pm & 3–6.30pm. Admission charge.

Igreja de Santa Maria (Church of St Mary)

This 16th-century church was almost entirely restored in the 19th century.

The finest features of the interior are the 18th-century wooden statues, including one of São Gonçalo, patron saint of Lagos. It was from the Manueline window of the church that King Sebastião is said to have roused his troops and bid a last farewell to the people of Lagos.

Praça da República. Open: Mon–Sat 8am–7.30pm, Sun for services only. Free admission.

Igreja de Santo António (Church of St Antony)

The sober façade of this small church hides the Algarve's most exuberant ecclesiastical interior. Known as 'the Golden Chapel', it has a profusion of carved and gilded woodwork, surrounding scenes from the life of St Antony. Miraculously, the main body of the church survived the 1755 earthquake, though the beautifully painted vaulted ceiling was rebuilt.

Rua General Alberto de Silveira. Open: Tue–Sun 9.30am–12.30pm &

NEARBY BEACHES

The main beach is the long exposed stretch of Meia Praia, northwest of the centre. More picturesque and sheltered (and crowded too) are the cove beaches west of town, tucked under golden cliffs. For coastal scenery, you cannot beat Ponta da Piedade, a promontory where cliff erosion has produced free-standing pillars, stacks and arches. From the cliff top, you can walk down a path to the grottoes. Alternatively, you can go all the way in a boat from the Lagos waterfront.

The Lagos city walls

2–5pm. Closed: Mon & holidays.
Admission charge.

Mercado dos Escravos (Slave Market)
On the Praça da República, an arcade
beneath the Lagos Customs House
marks the original site of the only slave
market in Portugal. During the days of
the great discoveries, hapless individuals
were brought back from Africa to Lagos
and sold off at this site. Today, the
arcade has a happier function: it acts as
an open-air art gallery.

Museu Regional de Lagos
(Regional Museum of Lagos)
Adjoining the Igreja de Santo António,
this small museum is devoted to
archaeology, ethnography and
religious art. A section displaying
pots, coins, Roman mosaics and other
local finds is followed by Algarvian
lobster pots, fishing nets and farming
tools, plus a few freak animal foetuses,
including a two-headed cat and a
one-eyed sheep.
Rua General Alberto de Silveira.
Tel: 282 762301. Open: Tue–Sun
9.30am–12.30pm & 2–5pm.
Closed: Mon & public holidays.
Admission charge; free Sun.

Lagos is 19km (12 miles) west of Portimão,
34km (21 miles) northeast of Sagres.

Aljezur
Lying between the sea and the
mountains of western Algarve, Aljezur
is a small town spread below the
ruins of its 10th-century sandstone
fortress. The remains, reached via steep
streets through the Moorish quarter,
provide a fine panorama of the
surrounding countryside.

Bridge over the Aljezur River

While in town, stop by the **Municipal Museum** to view collections from local archaeological digs, dating as far back as 7000 BC.

Proximity to peaceful beaches is one of the town's attractions. To the northwest, Amoreira and Monte Clérigo lie either side of a silted-up estuary and both have large expanses of empty sands. At Arrifana, 10km (6 miles) southwest of Aljezur, a big beach makes up for the drab village set on the cliffs above.

Some 17km (11 miles) north of Aljezur, the remote but picturesque little village of Odeceixe marks the last stop before the Algarve gives way to the Alentejo.

Aljezur is on the N120, 30km (19 miles) northwest of Lagos. Tourist office: Largo do Mercado. Tel: 282 998229. Open: summer Tue–Thur 9am–1pm & 2–5pm, Fri–Mon 9am–1pm & 2–5.30pm; winter Tue–Thur 9.30am–5pm, Fri–Mon 9.30am–1pm & 2–5.30pm.

Sagres

On the wild and windswept Sagres peninsula, turbulent seas pound against the cliffs. The land is parched, while the trees are stunted and bent from the unrelenting Atlantic gales. Perhaps it is not surprising that this southwesterly tip of Europe was once thought to be the *Fim do Mundo*, the 'End of the World'.

The Romans called Sagres the Sacrum Promontorium, or Sacred Promontory, and the only buildings found here then were shrines dedicated to the gods. In the 8th century, when the Muslims invaded Iberia, the relics of St Vincent, the 4th-century Christian martyr, were brought here for safekeeping. According to legend, sacred ravens kept a permanent vigil over the spot where the bones of the martyr were hidden, and when these relics were transferred to Lisbon, four centuries later, the birds flew with the ship all the way.

It was in the town of Sagres that Henry the Navigator set up his famous school of navigation ('school' in the sense of a group working together, not as in teaching), gathering cartographers, mariners and astronomers to set Portugal at the forefront of the Age of Discovery.

Today, Sagres is little more than a fishing village made up of squat white houses. The liveliest and most colourful spot is the harbour where the lobster boats arrive and offload their catch, destined for the market and local restaurants. The seas around Sagres, and off the southwest coast, provide some of the best fishing grounds in Portugal. Boats laden with tackle and bait can be hired by the day. Alternatively, you can take a boat trip to see the coast and nearby grottoes.

Beaches

The beaches of Sagres are windy and the seas can be rough. The Praia do Martinhal, 4km (2^1/2 miles) northeast of Sagres, is the most appealing, particularly if you like windsurfing. More sheltered is the pretty little beach of Beliche, below a converted fortress, on the road to Cabo de São Vicente.

Fortaleza (Fort)

The walls of this huge fortress loom on the rocky headland at the southern tip of the Sagres peninsula. Today, the most striking thing about the fortress is its setting, and the awesome circuit of walls skirting huge cliffs above dramatic seas. The original buildings were destroyed in part by Sir Francis Drake ('the English pirate' according to local brochures) who raided this coast in 1587 when Portugal was under Spanish occupation. Further devastation resulted from the earthquake of 1755. The latest damage inflicted on the site has been the destruction of some of the older buildings within the walls to make way for a modern box-like navigational museum, and the cementing over of the old stone walls. The scandal had national repercussions, with the president ordering a public inquiry.

From Henry the Navigator's era, only a small white-domed chapel survives, and this is always shut. Possibly original, too, is the gigantic *rosa dos ventos*, or

The giant wind compass, Sagres Fort

wind compass, which was discovered under a church in the 1920s and now stands to the left of the entrance.

From the tip of the promontory, where the red-topped lighthouse sits, you can watch fishermen dangling their long lines into the deep blue seas below. Mists permitting, you can see the lighthouse of Cabo de São Vicente to the west and the coastline as far as Lagos to the east.

Fort. Tel: 282 620140. Open: May–Sept daily 10am–8.30pm; Oct–Apr daily 10am–6.30pm. Admission charge.

Vila do Bispo

Some 9km (6 miles) northeast of Sagres, Vila do Bispo is a crossroads village with hilltop windmills and cafés serving *percebes* (barnacles), the local speciality. The parish church is decorated with particularly fine 18th-century *azulejos*.

Sagres is 33km (21 miles) southwest of Lagos on the N125 and N268. Tourist office: Rua Comandante Matoso. Tel: 282 624873. Open: Tue–Sat 9am–12.30pm & 1.30–5.30pm.

Cabo de São Vicente (Cape St Vincent) and beaches

By driving 6km (4 miles) over the wind-battered plateau from Sagres, you will reach Cape St Vincent, which marks the most southwesterly tip of continental Europe. From the lookout point to the right of the lighthouse, there are views of freighters and tankers rounding the Cape, and

Beach at Cabo de São Vicente

beyond them a seemingly endless ocean. The beam of the **lighthouse** is one of the most powerful in Europe, visible from a distance of 90km (56 miles). If the lighthouse is open, you can climb up the spiral staircase to see the prisms and 3,000-watt bulbs. Outside, stalls sell fishermen's socks and sweaters to tourists shivering in T-shirts and shorts. Despite the wind, Cape St Vincent is one of the best places in southern Portugal to see wild flowers. In addition, huge numbers of migrating birds are to be found in March/April and September/October.

The wild beaches of the west coast of the Algarve are very different in character from those of the developed south coast. Wind, strong waves and difficult access keep away all but avid surfers and backpackers, leaving these dramatic beaches practically untouched by tourism. The first and most accessible beach, heading north from Sagres, is the Praia do Castelejo. This is well signposted from Vila do Bispo. En route, the Torre de Aspa, a natural rock formation, soars to 150m (492ft). At the beach great rollers crash on to the sands and rocks. Watch them from the beach bar (where the *arroz de peixe* – fish with rice – is particularly good) or walk the cliff tops for spectacular sea views.

Further up the coast, at the beaches of Amado and Bordeira, the sands, surf and cliffs are staggeringly beautiful. Apart from surfers, all you are likely to see is a local goatherd coaxing his

flock along the cliffs. Both beaches are reached by dirt tracks, lined by dusty cacti and windblown fig trees. There are no signs, so follow your nose or ask a local.

Cabo de São Vicente lighthouse open: no official timetable – hours depend on the availability of the lighthouse keepers. Free admission.

Salema and Raposeira

Tucked away at the west end of the Algarve, the small village of **Salema** lies in the lee of the Sagres promontory. The main attraction here is the long sandy beach where the fishing community is still very much in evidence. In the early morning, you can watch fishermen untangling their nets or slicing squid by the side of their brightly coloured fishing smacks.

Up from the beach, on the east side, a jumble of white flat-roofed houses makes up the village. The narrow stone streets, where black-clad women gather in doorways, have plenty of local character.

To the west, and climbing up the slopes of the valley, the development is distinctly modern. The Salema Beach Club, a favourite British haunt, is a spreading complex of villas and apartments, with restaurants, swimming pools and bars.

Among the beach activities on offer are waterskiing, swimming, windsurfing and pedalos. Alternatively, you can take a trip along the coast in a fishing boat.

(*Cont. on p34*)

Henry the Navigator

The initiative behind Portugal's spate of maritime expeditions and discoveries, which began in the 15th century and led to the development of the vast Lusitanian empire, is traditionally credited to Prince Henry, 'the Navigator'. The third son of King João I, he was rewarded for his part in the capture of the North African stronghold of Ceuta, in 1415, with the dukedom of Viseu and governorship of the Algarve. In 1418, he moved from Viseu to Lagos and established a school of navigation, either in the city or near Sagres – the exact location is not known. The school attracted the finest cartographers, astronomers and navigators of the age, and contributed greatly to the improvement of navigational science.

A great many legends surrounding Henry are not supported by recent scholarship; some may result from mis-translation. The school and observatory, for example, which many accounts still claim he established to train navigators and mariners, was more like a 'school' of artists, not a training institution. And there is no evidence at all of an astronomical observatory, although they certainly observed the stars from there, and used celestial navigation.

None of which, of course, diminishes his accomplishments. Under his direction and with the expertise he gathered together at Sagres, the caravel – a lateen-sailed craft – was redesigned, making it lighter, faster and more responsive. That design allowed captains to undertake voyages that were never possible before.

He repeatedly defended Ceuta against Muslim attempts to recover it, he encouraged a disastrous attack on Tangier in 1437, and, as an old man, he fought at the famous victory at Alcácer-Ceguer.

Prince Henry also encouraged the settlement of the Atlantic islands. Madeira was discovered in 1419, the Azores in 1427 and the Cape Verde Islands in 1457.

Henry's motivation was at least threefold: religious zeal to firmly re-establish Christian control of Iberia (and stop the repeated coastal raids from Islamic bases in North Africa), establishing Portuguese commercial trade routes, and a desire to explore and expand the limits of the known world – and Portugal's part in it.

Profits from the trade went to finance more voyages – and to inspire mariners to risk venturing into the unknown. It was money that finally persuaded Gil Eanes to push around Cape Bojador, where so many of his predecessors had failed.

Henry's entire adult life was dedicated to these pursuits, and Portugal enjoyed the fruits of his work long after his death. By the time of his death, in 1460, Henry had managed to win the monopoly of all trade, including slavery, conducted along the African coast south of Cape Bojador, as well as a substantial percentage of the lucrative wheat and sugar trade by then operating out of Madeira.

Chapel and memorial to Henry the Navigator at Sagres

The Parque da Floresta golf course lies 3km (2 miles) inland, set in hilly countryside.

Raposeira is the village where Henry the Navigator once lived – or so local tradition has it. Villagers will point you in the direction of his so-called house. The village was also a resting place for medieval pilgrims who came all the way from Mértola (in the Alentejo) to worship the relics of St Vincent at Sagres. History aside, Raposeira is a pretty little village of old, gently decaying houses and winding streets and paths. Follow brown 'Megoliticos' signs south from Raposeira to find a cluster of megalithic sites.

On the road to Raposeira, 2km (1¼ miles) after Figueira, Nossa Senhora de Guadalupe is a delightful Romanesque/Gothic church, one of the Algarve's oldest, where Prince Henry is said to have prayed.

Some of the region's quietest beaches can be reached by taking the narrow and bumpy road south of Raposeira (signposted to Ingrina). Fork left for Zavial, which, when the tide is out, is a glorious beach. Ingrina (fork left) has a campsite and tends to be more crowded. The least accessible beach, Barranco João Vaz, is a favourite spot for naturists.

Salema is 17km (11 miles) northeast of Sagres and 22km (14 miles) west of Lagos.

Praia da Luz

Praia da Luz is one of the most appealing beach resorts in the Algarve. Situated at the quieter western end of the Algarve, the resort is made up of villas, pools and gardens, built around a crescent-shaped sandy bay with development spreading over the low western headland. Despite its growth, the town itself, Luz, is still a relaxed, peaceful place to stay. The emphasis is on beach life, sports and eating out at night. For a resort of its size, the sports facilities are impressive: windsurfing, sailing, waterskiing, diving, riding, tennis and squash.

Praia da Luz is 10km (6 miles) west of Lagos.

Burgau

The small resort of Burgau lies at the sleepy west end of the Algarve – sleepy, that is, until the old road leading to this end of the Algarve was rebuilt as a modern highway, destroying some of the natural beauty of the region in the process.

The crescent-shaped beach at Praia da Luz, one of the Algarve's best resorts

Although Burgau has doubled in size over the last decade, with an increasing number of mini-markets and tourist shops, it still manages to preserve much of its charm as a fishing village. Fishermen mending nets or painting boats provide plenty of local colour, and tourists and locals seem to mix well, either in the British-run pubs or in the fishermen's cafés, where fresh sardines are still grilled on tiny charcoal burners.

The tidy red-roofed cottages of old Burgau's centre sit on the slope above the port and beach, while newer developments and discos are kept at arm's length. The best way to reach the rocky beach, which almost completely disappears at high tide, is by walking down the narrow stone-paved street. There is rarely parking space at the tiny port, whose steep boat ramp is overlooked by several good restaurants. As an alternative, try the lovely Cabanas Velhas beach west of Burgau. There is also the swimming pool, available to visitors staying in Burgau. The centre of the resort is sprinkled with restaurants where the standard is generally good.

Just outside the village is the British-run Burgau Sports Centre (*rua Bela Vista. Tel: 282 697350*), offering excellent facilities for tennis, squash, volleyball and five-a-side football. Buy a drink or two and you are welcome to use the pool free of charge. Once a week the club organises a barbecue and folk night, with dancers from nearby Budens.

Burgau is 18km (11 miles) west of Lagos.

Whitewashed houses, terracotta tiles and cobbled streets in Burgau

Portimão

A major fishing port and industrial centre, Portimão is the largest and busiest town in the Algarve. It has no ancient monuments or in-town beach, so not many tourists come to this large and busy centre.

There are, however, several plus points to Portimão: they include one of the best shopping centres in the Algarve, the sardine cafés by the harbour, the bustling street life and – the most recent addition – a spectacular modern suspension bridge across the Arade River. Situated on the outskirts of the town, with splendid views of the (*Cont. on p38*)

Tour: Around Portimão

Portimão lies between the estuaries of two major rivers, the Alvor and the Arade, an area with fascinating evidence of earlier inhabitants – a Roman villa at Abicada and a Neolithic burial chamber at Alcalar. A visit to the Museu Regional in Lagos is essential to help interpret the sites. You can combine this tour with the Ferragudo walk (see pp40–41).

Allow 4 hours.

From Portimão town centre, take the new dual carriageway south to Praia da Rocha and then follow the coast road past a series of beaches and resorts to Alvor.

1 Alvor

This fishing village on the Alvor estuary is historic rather than pretty, but it has a good selection of restaurants. Worth visiting is the fish market (*lota*) and the interesting parish church which overlooks the harbour. At low tide, you can see villagers wading on to the sandbanks – the habitat of black-winged stilts, terns and other wetland birds – to collect shellfish (*see also p39*).
From Alvor, head back towards the N125 northwards, passing a small airport, a modern church and a casino. At the next junction, turn left, passing Le Meridien Penina Golf and Resort, turning left again after 4km (2¹/₂ miles) at the crossroads opposite Figueira. Bear right at the fork and then left up a narrow track by the Vila Arcolris. Cross the railway line and follow a line of cypress

trees which leads past the base of a ruined fort overgrown with trees.

2 Vila Abicada

The road ends at a group of white farm buildings to the side of which lie the remains of the Roman Vila Abicada, with substantial areas of mosaic intact. Although there have been plans to restore the site, funds are not available, so the fine mosaic floors in geometric designs are being invaded by grass. It was an extensive home of about 30 rooms, obviously of an important and wealthy figure, and the polychrome mosaics are in two peristyles, one of them hexagonal. The villa dates from the 4th century, and most of the excavated finds are now in the Museu Regional in Lagos.
Retrace your route to the N125.
If you wish to detour through the quaint village of Mexilhoeira Grande, turn left on to the N125, then right. Mexilhoeira Grande has an interesting parish church with two side doors decorated with 16th-century Manueline carvings.

If you do not take this detour, cross the N125 and drive through Figueira, continuing north through a valley of orchards. Pass through Poio and turn left at the next junction. After less than 1km (²/₃ mile), turn right.

3 Tumulus de Alcalar

The Tumulus de Alcalar is a megalithic grave of the *tholoi* type – that is, a chamber and corridor – and dates from the period 2,000–600 BC. A 19th-century engraving of a cross section of the tomb, together with relics found during its excavation, can be seen in the Museu Regional in Lagos. A small visitor centre at the entrance sells an excellent little guide to the site (€1).

Return to the road but continue straight ahead for Torre at the first junction, passing a wayside crucifix on the right and an agricultural aqueduct. Drive under a narrow railway bridge and, after less than 1km (²/₃ mile), rejoin the N125 almost opposite Penina. Turn left to return to Portimão.

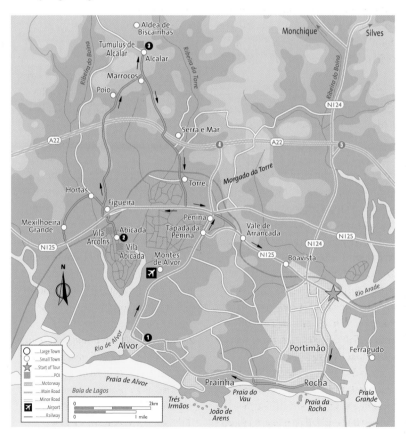

Tour: Around Portimão

Igreja Matriz in Portimão

estuary, the new bridge takes all the through traffic.

The town's main attraction used to be watching the fishing boats unload at the harbour, and now that this has moved to a newer facility the area is home to the excursion boats, including a two-masted sailing ship that takes passengers to the sea caves nearby. Their kiosks and quays, as well as those for pleasure yachts, are along the park-like promenade that borders a broad plaza filled with outdoor cafés.

Inland from the harbour, the streets are always full of shoppers. Not far from the main church, the pedestrianised Rua do Comércio and

the Rua Vasco da Gama are the principal shopping streets, selling fashionable clothes, food, furniture and all things Portuguese. In the rather more elegant Rua Santa Isabel, trendy boutiques and a stylish art gallery occupy the ground floors of some of the town's finer houses. The old fish market in the centre has been turned into a gallery for contemporary art, while a new fish market – one of the best in the Algarve – is located to the west of the centre.

By late morning, the wafting smell of charcoal-grilled fish permeates the streets, and the café-style restaurants on the waterside begin to fill. Here, the dish of the day, every day, is the simple sardine, eaten alfresco with salad and a jug of wine. In more sophisticated places you can try fish soups, fish risottos or freshly grilled bream, bass, swordfish and *peixe espada*, the long skinny 'scabbard fish', which has a pointed snout and silvery scales.

Boat excursions

Yachts moored in the harbour offer coastal trips and big-game cruisers lure in fishing enthusiasts with their advertisements featuring spectacular photographs of sharks. Even if the sharks don't bite, there are plenty of sea bass, conger eels and ray. The cruisers are fully equipped with fighting chairs, big-game rods, and the latest sonar systems which can detect fish up to a distance of 57km (35 miles). No experience is necessary. Among the game species regularly caught are the blue shark, the copper shark and the streamlined mako, which is renowned for its speed, fighting instincts and sensational leaps from the sea. Rather more tasty than other local sharks, it has been known to turn up on tourists' plates, under the guise of swordfish.

Igreja Matriz (Parish Church)

Dominating the centre of Portimão, the parish church was rebuilt after earthquake devastation. The finest surviving feature of the original church is the portico.

Largo da Igreja. Open: daily 9am–noon & 6–7pm.

Largo 1° de Dezembro (1st of December Square)

The tiles on the benches in this small park are well worth studying because they vividly illustrate ten crucial episodes in Portuguese history. The name of the park refers to 1 December 1640, the date that marked the end of 60 years of Spanish rule.

Portimão is 62km (39 miles) west of Faro and 18km (11 miles) east of Lagos. Tourist office: Avenida Zeca Afonso. Tel: 282 470732. Open: Mon & Fri 9.30am–12.30pm & 2–7pm, Tue–Thur 9.30am–8pm, Sat, Sun & off-season 9.30am–12.30pm & 2–5.30pm.

Alvor

Lying between Lagos and Portimão, Alvor consists of a picturesque hilltop fishing village and, well over 1km (²⁄₃ mile) away, a huge stretch of exposed beach dominated by dreary tower blocks. In the village, the tightly packed houses jostle around the parish church and slope down to the estuary quayside where the fishermen gather.

Next to the church's side door is a remnant of Moorish Algarve, the domed cube-shaped chapel of São Pedro, converted from a Muslim *marabout* (holy place).
Alvor is 8km (5 miles) west of Portimão and 18km (11 miles) east of Lagos.

Walk: Ferragudo beaches

Between Ferragudo and the hamlet of Seismarias, to the east, a series of red, green and blue arrows has been painted on walls along the roadside indicating three lengthy walks around the lanes and the coast. This walk follows part of the red route (in reverse), which includes the village of Ferragudo itself. If you do the whole route on foot, the total distance is about 9km (6 miles).

Allow 2 hours.

Start in Ferragudo, parking alongside the Igreja da Nossa Senhora on Largo Marcelino Franco.

1 Igreja da Nossa Senhora

The Igreja da Nossa Senhora is an attractive church with a statue of the Virgin and Child in a niche on the south wall. Opposite stands a monument in the shape of an anchor and a portrait of Lord Baden-Powell, commemorating the foundation of Ferragudo's Sea Scout group, No 413.

From here, you can walk, or drive, south following signs to the Praia Grande, passing the Cruzeiro da Senhora da Conceição, where the road approaches the coast, and the Praia da Angrinha beach near a junction of several roads. Take the lane to the right.

2 Castelo de São João de Arade

The lane leads to the handsome Castelo de São João de Arade, overlooking the river from its headland. Built in the 17th century to guard the estuary – together with the Forte de Santa Catarina on the opposite bank – it has been a private residence since its restoration from ruins by the poet Coelho de Carvalho.

Return to the road junction and follow the first lane right to Praia Grande.

3 Praia Grande

As its name (Great Beach) suggests, this is indeed a long sweep of sand, whose waters are protected from the Atlantic waves by the *molhe* (seawall) to the south, and which has become known in the Algarve as one of the best beaches for windsurfing. You can buy or hire equipment at the beach, and there are several popular bars and restaurants. Walk north along the sand for another view of the castle.

Walk along the full length of the beach (the sand can be very soft) and scramble up the cliffs to walk along the cliff tops to the molhe.

4 Praia do Molhe

This small beach lies on either side of the long *molhe* that juts out into the Arade estuary almost meeting another seawall coming from the Portimão side. You can walk out along the wall, a favourite place for fishermen.

Walk along the lane leading away from the beach and turn right to make the short descent to another sheltered sandy beach, the Praia do Pintadinho. This also has a beach restaurant and larger waves, being on the Atlantic, rather than the Arade. To avoid having to retrace your steps, it is possible to climb up to the cliffs near the lighthouse to reach the Ponta do Altar.

5 Ponta do Altar

The Ponta do Altar is the southwestern-most point on the Ferragudo coast, and is guarded by an inhabited lighthouse (*farol*). From the lighthouse, there are views across the *molhe* to Portimão. You can walk east along the cliff top – again meeting the occasional red arrow, pointing in the opposite direction to the way you are going – with views to the beaches below.

You may search among the low gorse bushes for the tiny snails (*caramujos*), which are a local delicacy.

The path crosses a valley, past a new villa development, before joining the lane that leads down to the Praia dos Caneiros.

6 Praia dos Caneiros

You will pass a small restaurant in the lane and there is another on the beach itself. The sand is backed by the usual golden sandstone cliffs with low arches beginning to be eroded at their base. At low tide, you can walk around the small western headland to another bay, the Praia dos Torrados.

From the Praia dos Caneiros, it is a 3.5km (2-mile) walk back to Ferragudo along the lane, continuing straight over at the crossroads that leads left to the molhe.

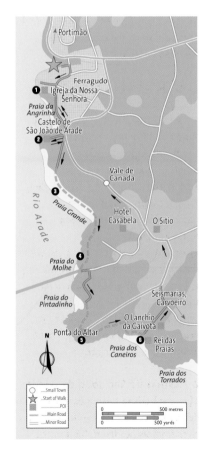

Sunset over Praia da Rocha

Praia da Rocha

The pioneer resort of the Algarve, Praia da Rocha has been receiving tourists since the 1930s. Anyone who knew the resort in those days would find it hard to recognise today. From one elegant hotel and a handful of villas it has grown into an international resort with scores of modern hotels, bars and souvenir shops.

The prime attraction is, and always has been, the beach. This looks entirely natural, though in fact the sands were imported from nearby Portimão when the harbour was dredged. The wide band of flat golden beach, backed by high sandstone cliffs, stretches for 2km (1^1/$_4$ miles). Wind and water erosion have left freakish rock formations along the beach, sculpted into arches, tunnels and – if you use your imagination – shapes resembling animals and human beings.

Well above the beach, the cliff-top promenade runs eastwards as far as the fortress of Santa Catarina, built to defend Portimão. Today, café tables are laid out within the fort and tourists can take advantage of the views across the estuary of the Arade River and down to the jetty, where anglers cast their lines. From the western headland, the views of the coastline are even more spectacular.

Praia da Rocha's first hotel was the Bela Vista, converted from an early 20th-century mansion with Moorish overtones. Today, it looks incongruous amid the modern concrete.

From Praia da Rocha, you can take a boat westwards along the coast to Praia dos Três Irmãos. Alternatively, you can walk there along the cliff top. Either way, there are excellent views of the rugged cliffs and rock stacks.

Praia da Rocha is 2km (1^1/$_4$ miles) south of Portimão and 64km (40 miles) west of Faro.

Tourist office: Avenida Tomás Cabreira. Tel: 282 419132. Open: Mon & Fri 9.30am–12.30pm & 2–7pm or 8pm, Tue–Thur 9.30am–8pm, Sat, Sun & off-season 9.30am–12.30pm & 2–5.30pm.

Serra de Monchique

The Serra de Monchique, forming a natural boundary between the Algarve and the Alentejo, is a thickly wooded mountain range covered with cork oak, eucalyptus, chestnut and pine. The lush and varied vegetation has given it the name of 'the garden of the Algarve'. The hillside roads are bordered by mimosas, wild rhododendrons and the *Arbutus unedo* tree, whose strawberry-like berries are the main ingredient of *medronho*, the locally made, fiery liqueur.

The scenery and the views, combined with the attractions of a spa village and a hill town, make Monchique one of the Algarve's most popular tourist excursions. Don't be surprised, therefore, if a coach descends mid-morning on the Caldas de Monchique, spilling out tourists and temporarily disturbing the tranquillity of this pretty spot in the valley.

Caldas de Monchique

The centuries-old spa town of Caldas de Monchique lies in a quiet, wooded valley, 250m (820ft) above the coastline. The medicinal waters, discovered by the Romans, are said to do wonders for rheumatism, skin diseases, convulsions and indigestion. Even so, the dropsy-ridden King João II found their therapeutic value questionable when, in 1495, he bathed at Monchique (albeit against medical advice) and died shortly afterwards in Alvor. There are eight springs

altogether, which produce 20 million litres of water a year, and if you don't take the waters here you are bound to taste them in bottled form somewhere along the Algarve.

Focusing on its main square, the resort consists of a cluster of upmarket hotels, shops and restaurants, all of which have been restored in recent years, and almost all of which belong to the **Monchique Termas Company** (*www.monchiquetermas.com*). Overlooking the square is a converted casino, which looks like a Moorish palace. Gambling was popular with the Spanish bourgeoisie who frequented the Caldas de Monchique in the mid-19th century. The former casino is now an exhibition centre. Apart from water, Monchique is famous for *medronho* liqueur made from arbutus fruit and distilled in copper. Be prepared for the kick; the *medronho* made locally is 90° proof.

Beyond the square, a babbling brook tumbles down the hillside. Stone picnic benches are laid out in the shade of the waterside trees. From here, there are lovely walks through the woods. Down the hill from the main square, you can try a whole range of water treatments at the Termal Hotel.

Monchique

The market town of Monchique lies 7km (4 miles) north of the Caldas, overlooking a valley of orchards and woods. It is traditionally a handicrafts centre and along the approach road

Chairs painted with bright floral designs for sale in Monchique

you can see stalls selling basketry and pottery.

Formerly a pretty mountain village, Monchique has expanded somewhat inelegantly, the outskirts typified by dull modern architecture and by bulldozers, which continue to carve up the hillsides. However, the narrow, stone-paved alleys of the centre, a few still lined with elegant 18th-century houses, are well worth exploring. Moreover, the views from the upper levels of the town are breathtaking.

Every month (on the third Friday) Monchique is the scene of a huge agricultural fair when all the local farmers gather to trade their livestock.

The main church in Monchique, the **Igreja Matriz**, is famous for its extraordinary Manueline portal. The carved twisted columns, resembling

cables of rope, radiate out into nautical knots, creating a striking effect against the plain white façade of the church.

The interior, kept immaculately, has three naves supported by pillars with Manueline capitals and a fine wooden ceiling, while blue, white and yellow *azulejos* decorate the lower side walls of the church (*Rua da Igreja. Open: Mon–Fri 10am–noon*).

Monchique environs

The grey neglected Convento da Nossa Senhora do Desterro (Convent of Our Lady of Sorrows), surrounded by camellias and weeds, perches above the town and can only be reached on foot. It is no more than a shell but it is one that commands a superb sweep of the Serra de Monchique, giving way to the coast below. The best views are from the bell tower, but watch out for falling debris as you go.

West of Monchique the road snakes up the side of the **Fóia mountain** through woods of eucalyptus and pine, which soon give way to scrub and moorland. Along the wayside, flower-decked restaurants tempt you with their sweeping views over hills and valleys to the coast and their alfresco meals of smoked ham and chicken *piri-piri*. Hidden on the hillsides are the villas and pools of an expatriate British community who, no doubt anticipating the tidal wave of tourism on the coast, built villas on the quiet slopes of Fóia in the 1950s and 1960s.

The peak of Fóia, which you expect to be totally deserted, is scarred by TV masts, tourist shops and hawkers. Stallholders do a roaring trade in chunky sweaters, sold to tourists caught unawares by the cold gusts on the peak.

Provided that there is no mist or heat haze, the views will make your trip worthwhile. The peak, at 902m (2,959ft), is the highest in the Algarve, and on a clear day you can see the foothills stretching all the way to Cabo de São Vicente (Cape St Vincent).

The peak of **Picota**, rising to the southeast of Monchique, has equally good, if not better, views, despite its more modest height (773m/2,536ft). There is no proper road to the top, but the hike up is well worth the effort.

Caldas de Monchique is 18km (11 miles) north of Portimão. Monchique town is 25km (16 miles) north of Portimão. Tourist office: Tel: 282 911189. www.cm-monchique.pt. Open: Mon–Fri 9.30am–1pm & 2–5.30pm.

Silves

It is hard to believe that this sleepy backwater, beside the Arade River, was once a sumptuous Moorish stronghold. As the capital of what was then called al Gharb, Silves was described by one historian as 'stronger and ten times more remarkable than Lisbon'. Likened to Baghdad, it was a city of mosques, bazaars and orchards full of citrus fruits. Ships used to come up the Arade River, anchor at the port, and load up with lemons, oranges, figs and cork.

In 1189, Sancho I brought this lavish stronghold to its knees. Furthering his anti-Muslim military campaign, he persuaded the Crusaders to help him expel the Moors from the citadel of Silves. The Moors held out for many months, but when there was no more water or food they were forced to surrender. Despite Sancho's protestations, the Crusaders then plundered the castle, torturing and murdering the departing Moors.

Silves was recaptured by the Moors two years later but the writing was on the wall for Arab hegemony in the Algarve. By 1249, the capital had finally fallen, along with Faro and the remaining Moorish footholds in the region.

(*Cont. on p48*)

Silves – the central square

Fishing

The Phoenicians are given the credit for first noting the annual migration of the tunny, or tuna fish, from the open waters of the Atlantic to the inshore waters of the Algarvian coast. Traditionally, the fish were caught in large traps, harpooned and then dragged on deck. The struggles between man and fish, which can grow as large as 450kg (992lb), were so bloody that they were dubbed 'bullfights of the sea'. Today, the tunny population is much diminished, and the catch, using modern methods such as sonar to locate the fish, takes place in foreign waters.

The fishing industry in general has seen a downward spiral in recent years. Dwindling fish stocks, soaring fuel prices, old-fashioned fishing boats and intense international competition have all contributed to the decline. About a quarter of the fish in Portugal is now imported –

The bow of a fishing boat on the beach at Albufeira

The fishing village of Ferragudo

there are even sardines from Russia! The EU has committed around €300 million to the Portuguese fishing industry over the next six years, and the Portuguese have renewed fishing rights in Moroccan waters, so hopefully the tide will turn. Meanwhile, there are still little ports where you can see the coloured smacks offloading their catch in the early morning, and backstreets and beaches where you still catch wafts of local sardines, sizzling on charcoal braziers.

A curious legacy of Algarve fishing traditions is the Algarvian *cão d'água* (water dog). This is a curly-haired, poodle-like creature, whose webbed paws and love of the water made it a great boon to the fishermen. The dogs were trained to guide fish into nets, bark in the fog, and swim from boat to boat with messages. They were also reputed to have saved many men from drowning. Today, these dogs are quite rare, but a programme has been devised to try to save the breed (*see p70*).

Silves gradually slipped into oblivion. By the late 16th century, the bishopric of the Algarve had moved from here to Faro and the population of this former capital was reduced to a mere 140.

The fruit trees still flourish in modern Silves, but the Arade River is silted up and has been for centuries. The most prominent reminder of Silves' illustrious past is the noble shell of the Moorish fortress that crowns the town. Within the walls, the gardens provide an oasis of peace, except during the third week of July, when the castle becomes the venue for an international beer festival.

Beneath its castle, Silves is a small and unassuming town of steep cobbled streets and red-roofed white- and pastel-washed houses. Bringing this ancient Moorish capital into the 21st century is the new university.

Castelo (Castle)

The great circuit of turreted castle walls dominates the town. The steep cobbled Rua da Sé leads up, past the cathedral, to the arched gateway of the castle. Within the walls cats doze in the shade of jacaranda and apricot trees while stallholders sell linen and lace. The monumental bronze statue of Sancho I, inscribed 'King of Portugal, Silves and the Algarve', evokes memories of less tranquil days.

The castle battlements command sweeping views of Silves and the surrounding hills, covered in orange and lemon trees. Below you, to the south, is one of the town's last surviving cork factories. More immediately below are the old silos and the dark depths of the Cistern of the Dogs, created from an ancient copper mine and well worth descending into. An underground passage once linked the cistern to the Arade River and water was drawn up in clay buckets.

Largo do Castelo. Tel: 282 440800. Open: winter daily 9am–5.30pm; summer daily 9am–8pm. Admission charge. Restoration is currently taking place at the castle and gardens but is not affecting opening hours.

Cruz de Portugal (Cross of Portugal)

On the outskirts of town, this carved cross, in a little pavilion, dates from the 16th century. It is 3m (10ft) tall and carved from limestone. One side depicts the Crucifixion, the other the Descent from the Cross. From this side of town there are excellent views of the fortress.

On the N124 towards São Bartolomeu de Messines.

Museu Municipal de Arqueologia (Municipal Archaeology Museum)

This innovative museum focuses on a beautifully preserved 12th-century Moorish well, which was discovered in 1979. During the excavation of the well, the diggers unearthed a wealth of artefacts, including ceramics, square Moorish coins and jewellery. Other exhibits, dating from the prehistoric era to the 17th century, include a carved head, which probably came from a Greek temple, Roman carvings, and Phoenician and Visigoth pottery. *Rua das Portas de Loulé 14. Tel: 282 444832. Open: Mon–Sat (except holidays) 9am–5.30pm. Admission charge.*

Sé de Santa Maria (Cathedral of Our Lady)

Lying in the shadow of the castle, this cathedral is one of the Algarve's very few Gothic monuments. Like the rest of Silves, it has suffered the ravages of time and undergone heavy restoration, but the dignified interior, with its lofty aisles and nave, is impressive nevertheless. Among the finest features are the tombs, some of which may belong to the Crusaders who helped capture Silves from the Moors.

Largo da Sé. Tel: 282 442325. Open: daily 9am–5.30pm in summer. Closes at 1pm Sun. Free admission (voluntary contribution).

Silves is 17km (11 miles) northeast of Portimão, on the N124. Tourist office: Rua 25 de Abril, off the Praça do Município. Tel: 282 442255. Open: summer daily 9.30am–7pm; off-season Mon–Sat 9.30am–1pm & 2–5.30pm, Sun 9am–noon.

Lagoa

Not to be confused with the larger town of Lagos, Lagoa lies on the main road east of Portimão. It is a small, unpretentious town, known first and foremost as the Algarve's chief producer of wine.

The parish church of Lagoa, set in an immaculate cobbled square

There is nothing very remarkable about the town of Lagoa itself, though you can still find plenty of local atmosphere in the backstreets, particularly in the tiny *tasca* bar-cum-grocery stores where the locals knock back Lagoan wines amid strings of hanging onions and crates of oranges. The town's main sight is the parish church with its restored Baroque façade.

In the big **Cooperativa** on the main road, you can taste Lagoan wines and watch the processes of cork-fitting and label-pasting, still done by hand. Red wines predominate, but there is also a Lagoan white, a rosé and a golden sherry-like aperitif wine. Tasters should be wary of the high alcohol content of Lagoan wines – 13 or 13.5° is quite normal.

The Lagoa Wine Cooperativa is on the Portimão road. Tel: 282 342181. Open: Mon–Fri 9.30am–noon & 2–6pm. Free admission, but you pay if you taste the wines. Book 24 hours ahead.

Aqualand

Located near Lagoa in Alcantarilha, this is one of several water parks in the area, boasting mega-slides, wave pools and areas for all ages.

Apartado 11, 8365-908 Alcantarilha. Tel: 282 322828. www.aqualand.pt. Open: end May–mid-Sept 10am–6pm. Admission charge.

Tumbling rocks lead down to a glittering sea at Carvoeiro

Porches

The potteries of Porches are to be found along the N125, 5km (3 miles) east of Lagoa. Here you can find everything from ceramic snails to ornate Algarvian chimney pots. For floral-patterned majolica, based on traditional designs, try Porches Pottery (on the south side of the main road). Here you can watch the pots and plates being painted by hand.

Lagoa is on the N125, 7km (4 miles) east of Portimão.

Carvoeiro

Carvoeiro is one of a string of overgrown fishing villages whose hills and headlands are now splashed with blindingly white villa constructions. Happily, though, the new development is restricted to the outskirts, leaving a centre which has a certain amount of colour and charm. Down by the beach the fishermen earn their living by taking tourists to the grottoes by day and fishing for sardines by night.

The beach, backed by ochre-coloured cliffs, is barely big enough to cope with the huge number of visitors that Carvoeiro now receives. The real beauty of this stretch of predominantly rocky coastline lies in its fascinating grottoes and secluded sandy coves. To the east of the resort lie the peaceful beaches of Marinha and Benagil (*see p52 & p53*), but the top attraction of the area lies just 1km (²/₃ mile) east of the centre, at Algar Seco.

Here, a long flight of steps takes you down to a beauty spot where the pitted ochre cliffs have been eroded to form dramatic stone arches and grottoes. Provided that the waves are not crashing against the cliffs, the waters – deep blue and transparent – provide a paradise for snorkellers. The *taverna* on the rocks makes a lovely spot for a snack or a sundowner.

Lying roughly halfway between Lagos and Albufeira, Carvoeiro makes a good base for exploring the western half of the Algarve. Silves, Portimão and Lagos are all within easy reach, and Monchique, in the mountains, makes a memorable excursion. For those who want to stay put, the centre of Carvoeiro is liberally endowed with cafés, bars, pubs and restaurants. The resort has two tennis courts, squash courts and a golf course.

Carvoeiro is 5km (3 miles) south of the N125, 13km (8 miles) east of Portimão. Tourist office: Praia do Carvoeiro. Tel: 282 357728. Open: Mon–Sat 9.30am–7pm (5pm off-season).

Armação de Pêra

Though the fishermen still haul their skiffs down the sands, Armação de Pêra looks a far cry from the fishing village it used to be. The huge development spreads along the coastline, its high-rise blocks overlooking what the resort itself claims is the biggest beach in the Algarve; true or not, it certainly is vast.

(*Cont. on p54*)

Walk: Praia da Marinha

This gentle walk of 5km (3 miles) combines quiet lanes with one of the most dramatic sections of the Algarve coast. There are several cafés and restaurants along the route, and you could extend your walk along unmarked, but well-defined, cliff-top paths in either direction – east to the cliff-top chapel of Senhora da Rocha or west to the Praia do Carvalho and Carvoeiro.

Allow 2 hours.

The start of the walk can be approached from either Carvoeiro or the N125. West of Porches, midway between Portimão and Albufeira, take the turning opposite the International School. Facing the sea (with several restaurants behind you), the building on the hill to the left is a wine factory (Fábrica Vinho): take the lane straight ahead, signposted Praia da Marinha.

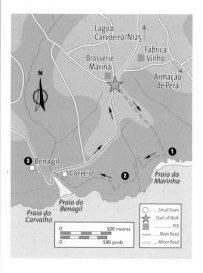

1 Praia da Marinha

In spring, the verges and low stone walls along this lane are dotted with wild flowers and the almond trees are in full pink and white blossom. After 1km (^{2}/₃ mile), passing a small group of houses, the road finishes at a large car park, where the house on the left has a particularly fine almond tree. To the left, a well-maintained stepped path leads past banks of cacti to the beach at Marinha – very popular in summer when you can eat hot or cold snacks on the wooden deck of its restaurant. *Returning to the car park, take the path leading west, across the cliffs, towards Benagil.*

2 The path to Benagil

In its early stretches, the sandstone cliffs have been eroded into unusual ridges; it is possible to walk out to the point overlooking the sea, but great care should be taken, since the cliff edges are extremely friable, and you may prefer to leave them to the seagulls. The next section is perhaps the most impressive – looking back towards Marinha you will see a solitary white villa sitting on the headland, with layers of ochre cliffs and stacks between. You can hear, but not always see, the waves crashing against the cliffs below you on to small, inaccessible beaches and into caves and blowholes.

Follow the path as it turns inland to cross a small, green valley and then climb up the other side to rejoin the cliffs.

3 Benagil

The headlands towards Benagil are broader, although the village itself remains hidden until the path turns inland and down a flight of steps next to the post office (*correio*). You can take the steep road left, down to the small beach and fishing harbour. From here, you can take one of the small boats that leave regularly in summer to tour the beaches and caves along the coast.

One beach that you can reach on foot is the Praia do Carvalho. Climb up to the other side of Benagil, where there are several more cafés and restaurants, and along the headland; the beach entrance is down a flight of steps cut into a tunnel in the rock. A single rock stack stands at the centre of this curved bay of deeply shelving sand and, on the far side, steps have been cut into the soft cliff face. In spring, it can be deserted; in summer, a beach café sells custard-filled doughnuts (*bolos*) and the sand is lined with sunbeds and parasols.

Caves eroded by the waves in the soft cliff face at Benagil

The lane back from Benagil to the car park climbs past the post office and more restaurants. It then passes scattered cottages where the old Algarve, of small plots of vines and a few hens, stands side by side with modern villas before returning to the junction at Brasserie Marina. On the lane leading to the wine factory stands a handsome, decaying Algarvian house.

To the east the wide band of golden sand is seemingly endless; to the west the beach gives way to curious rock formations with grottoes and small sandy coves, only accessible by fishing boat. One of the prettiest of the coves is Senhora da Rocha, about 2km (1¹/₄ miles) west of Armação de Pêra, which takes its name from the little Romanesque chapel perched on a rocky promontory above the glorious beach.

The new and ever-expanding development in Armação de Pêra has not entirely swallowed up the original village. In the centre, on the waterfront, are the ruins of an 18th-century fort with a small chapel dedicated to St Antony. Vestiges of the old fishing quarter survive, and you can still enjoy freshly caught fish and seafood in the cafés and restaurants.

Zoo Marine

Zoo Marine offers dolphin shows, marine exhibits, tropical and prey birds in a natural habitat, as well as a full range of amusement park rides.
On the N125 between Guia and Alcantarilha. The zoo operates a pick-up service from various points between Portimão and Quarteira. Tel: 289 560301. www.zoomarine.pt. Open: daily May–mid-Jun & Sept–Oct 10am–6pm; mid-Jun–Aug 10am–7.30pm; Nov–Apr 10am–5pm. Admission charge.

Armação de Pêra is 3km (2 miles) south of the N125 and about 47km (29 miles) *west of Faro. Tourist office: Avenida Marginal. Tel: 282 312145. Open: Mon–Fri 9.30am–12.30pm & 2–5.30pm, Sat & Sun 9.30am–5.30pm.*

Albufeira

From a quaint fishing village, Albufeira has grown into a giant cosmopolitan resort. Clinging to the cliffs above the main beach lies the old town, with its distinctive Moorish flavour. The narrow cobbled alleys, lined by whitewashed cottages, lead down to terraces overlooking the sea and the beach. Further proof that all is not destroyed is the Praia dos Barcos, or Fishermen's Beach, where brightly painted fishing boats are drawn up on the sands. At night you can see the lights of the sardine boats out at sea, and early in the morning you can watch the catch being auctioned at the old fish market.

Albufeira's monuments are limited to a handful of churches, including the chapel of the Misericórdia in the old town and the church of São Sebastião, with Manueline motifs on the portal.

The main beach lies below the town; access is through a tunnel under the Sol e Mar Hotel or down the cliffside steps. The sea here is safe for children. The less crowded beaches are São Rafael, 5km (3 miles) west, or Olhos de Água, 7km (4 miles) east.
Albufeira is 39km (24 miles) west of Faro and 52km (32 miles) east of Lagos. Tourist office: Rua 5 de Outubro.

The Algarve coast: beautiful sandy beaches and dramatic rocks

Tel: 289 585279. Open: mid-Jun–Aug Tue–Thur 9.30am–7pm, Fri–Mon 9.30am–1pm & 2–5.30pm; Sept–mid-Jun Mon–Fri 9.30am–1pm & 2–5.30pm.

Praia da Oura

Once an offshoot of Albufeira, Praia da Oura has grown to become a self-contained tourist resort. Main attractions are the sandy beach, non-stop nightlife and the bullring. *Praia da Oura is 2.5km (1¹/₂ miles) east of Albufeira centre.*

Alte

It is not surprising that numerous excursion coaches choose to stop at Alte on their inland tours. Perhaps a little too pristine to be typical of inland Algarve, it is a pretty village of streams and waterfalls, cobbled streets with freshly whitewashed houses, delicate laced chimneys and balconies brimming with flowers. The village has long been known for the purity of its springs, and for centuries people have been coming here to take the fountain waters.

Nowadays, the banks of the stream make popular picnic spots and, during the summer months, folklore evenings are held at the Fonte Pequena (Little Fountain Inn).

The finest features of Alte's parish church are the finely carved Manueline portico and – if you can get inside – the 18th-century *azulejos* and colourful religious statuary. The quaint Baroque chapel of São Luís stands on a small square at the other end of the village. The adjoining museum has a heterogeneous collection of cow bells, rat traps, old pots and photographs of the Alte town band in the 1930s.

Alte is on the N124, 11km (7 miles) east of São Bartolomeu de Messines.

Eastern Algarve

Long stretches of golden sand, upmarket resorts and a trio of small cities where local life predominates over tourism give the eastern Algarve an interesting variety. In place of the dramatic rock formations and little coves of the west, the eastern Algarve offers low rolling countryside that's perfect for golf courses, often ending at beaches that slope off gently into the sea, making this region a favourite with families with young children.

Towns look quite different from those perched on steep slopes between the rocky headlands of the western Algarve. Many of them are relatively flat and, instead of the open sea, face on to lagoons. These are protected by the long line of sandy islands that make up the Parque Natural da Ria Formosa.

Occupying over 50km (31 miles) of shoreline, from Faro to the Spanish border, this nature reserve is an ornithologist's haven. The marshland, salt pans and sandbars attract a huge variety of birdlife, both resident and migratory. Watch out in particular for waders, such as black-winged stilts, avocets, ruffs and little egrets.

Fishing boats still tie up along the picturesque river front by the arched bridge in Tavira and the long waterfront in Olhão; each of these has a picturesque market hall where the catch is sold each morning. Despite the decline in fishing, these markets and the fleets that keep them filled are still active, and the EU's commitment of €300 million to support the Portuguese fishing industry, plus the renewal of fishing rights in waters off North Africa, spell a brighter future for the fleet. While fishing may never again exceed tourism throughout the Algarve, in these eastern regions it is definitely holding strong.

The first view of the Algarve for many foreign visitors is this eastern section, as they arrive at Faro's international airport.

Faro

Capital of the Algarve since 1756, the city of Faro is the gateway by air to the whole region. Although its long history of sieges, raids and earthquakes has destroyed much of the old Roman and Moorish architecture, Faro remains a charming walled old town, perfect for strolling through its old quarter or shopping in the pedestrianised streets. Harbourside gardens shaded by tall trees provide a respite from the midday sun in the summer. Storks flying in and out of their unruly nests perched on

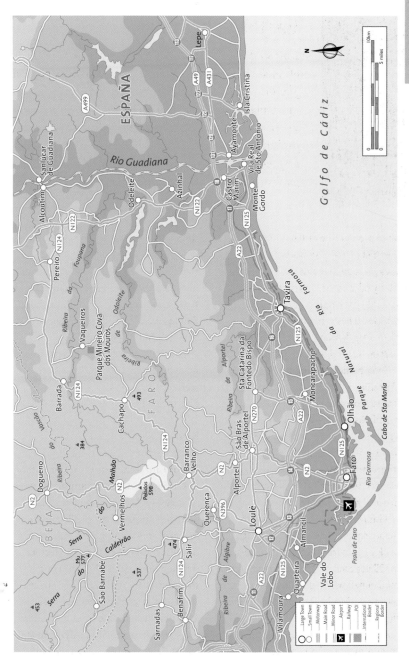

Eastern Algarve

Large Town
Small Town
Motorway
Main Road
Minor Road
Railway
Airport
JO1
International Border
Regional Border

ESPAÑA

Rio Guadiana

Golfo de Cádiz

Lepe
Isla Cristina
Ayamonte
Vila Real de Sto António
Monte Gordo
Castro Marim
Azinhal
Odeleite
Alcoutim
Santlúcar de Guadiana
Pereiro
Vaqueiros
Barrada
Parque Mineiro Cova dos Mouros
Cachopo
Dogueno
Malhão
Vermelhos
Pelados
Barranco Velho
São Brás de Alportel
Sta Catarina da Fontedo Bispo
Moncarapacho
Tavira
Olhão
Faro
Almancil
Loulé
Querença
Salir
Benafim
Sarnadas
São Barnabé
Alportel
Vale do Lobo
Quarteira
Vilamoura
Praia de Faro
Ria Formosa
Parque Natural do Ria Formosa
Cabo de Sta Maria

A499
N124
N122
N124
N124
N124
N270
N125
N396
N2
A22

Serra do Caldeirão
Serra do Mu
Ribeira do Vascão
Ribeira de Odeleite
Ribeira da Foupana
Ribeira de Alportel
Ribeira de Algibre

FARO
BEJA

rooftops and church towers add another charming touch to the old town centre.

Visitors to Faro in summer should make an early start as parking is notoriously difficult (try the area around the waterfront), and because sightseeing in the midday heat is extremely tiring.

Capela dos Ossos (Chapel of Bones)

Tucked behind the Igreja do Carmo is the gruesome Chapel of Bones, faced with some 1,250 bones and skulls of monks, dug up from the church graveyard when the chapel was built in 1816.

In the quiet courtyard behind the chapel is a small altar in a niche that is also lined with skulls and bones.
Open: Mon–Fri 10am–12.30pm & 2–5pm. Admission charge (pay in the sacristy of the Igreja do Carmo).

Igreja do Carmo (Carmelite Church)

Standing among blocks of modern flats in the Largo do Carmo square, the majestic twin-belfried façade of the Carmelite Church looks completely out of place. Even so, the interior of this fine Baroque church is profusely decorated with 18th-century gilded woodcarvings.

ALLIES AND EARTHQUAKES

Ironically, the worst damage was done by the English, long-standing allies of the Portuguese, when the Earl of Essex sacked the city (then under Spanish occupation) in 1596. Most of what was left was then wiped out by the catastrophic earthquake of 1755.

Largo do Carmo. Open: Mon–Fri 10am–12.30pm & 2–5pm, Sat 10am–1pm. Free admission.

Igreja de São Francisco (Church of St Francis)

Just west of the old town, the Igreja de São Francisco stands on a large open square. The exuberant gilded woodcarving, and the glazed tiles depicting scenes from the life of St Francis, provide a surprising contrast to the façade.
Largo de São Francisco. No official opening hours (ring the bell on the door to the left of the entrance). Free admission.

Igreja de São Pedro (Church of St Peter)

São Pedro is embellished with beautiful Baroque gilded woodwork and, in one of the chapels, *azulejo* tiles depicting the saint. The 16th-century church was built on the site of a fishermen's chapel.
Largo de São Pedro. Open: Mon–Fri 10am–1pm & 3–5pm. Free admission.

Museu Etnográfico Regional (Regional Ethnographic Museum)

Situated on the third floor of an austere public building, the Regional Ethnographic Museum is devoted to the traditional life of the Algarvians. Exhibits include tuna nets, chimney pots, beehives and basketry.
Rua do Pé da Cruz 4. Tel: 289 827610.

(Cont. on p62)

See pp60–61 for walk route

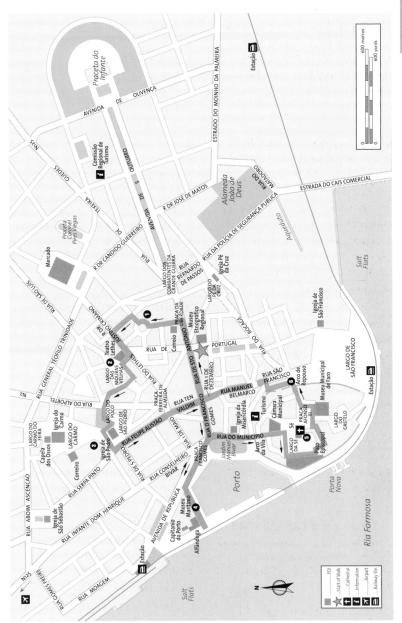

Walk: Faro

Despite its off-putting suburbs, Faro at heart is a lively place whose old quarter has one of the most elegant squares in the Algarve. This walking tour (see map on p59) is best done in the relative cool of the morning.

Allow 2 hours.

Start from the Praça da Liberdade, the commercial centre of town, next to the main car park. Leave the square, following Rua Dr João Lucio, passing a post office (correio) on the left, then turn left into Rua Muzinho de Albuquerque.

1 Rua Muzinho de Albuquerque

The streets in this area are named after Portuguese writers and poets, and the street signs, made of attractive tiles, give short biographical details of each. The area has some interesting buildings, including the astonishing Vivenda Mardlia, on the corner of Rua Almeida Garret, an ochre-coloured creation of fantastic decoration. At the end of the street, Alfarrabista is a bookshop in the old tradition with an extensive range of vintage books, postcards and magazines.

Turn left towards Rua Dr Justino Crimano, then left again to the small square dominated by the Ministry of Culture building, with its white façade and green windows.

2 Teatro Lethes

Formerly the Jesuit college of Santiago Maior, today this building houses occasional exhibitions – and one of the Algarve's greatest treasures, the Teatro Lethes. During office hours, enquire from the concierge if you can see the *teatro, faz favor*, and you should be escorted to the tiny ornate masterpiece – a reproduction in miniature of Milan's opera house, La Scala.

Cross Largo das Mouras Velhas and the gardens of Rua da Conceição. The bust you will see is of Portuguese writer Assis Esperança. Turn right up Rua do Sol. Cross Rua do Alportel and the Largo do Poço to enter the imposing Largo do Carmo.

3 Largo do Carmo

To one side is the Baroque Igreja do Carmo, the Carmelite Church, whose cemetery contains the macabre Capela dos Ossos (Chapel of Bones). Nearby is the smaller Igreja de São Pedro.

Take Rua Filipe Alistão – looking out for

the traditional grocer's store at No 26 – and cross the small square to reach the busy pedestrianised shopping streets that lead to the harbour. Turn right for Praça Francisco Gomes and the palm trees of the Jardim Manuel Bivar.

4 Museu Marítimo

For the best view of the harbour, walk out to the Museu Marítimo (Maritime Museum). The harmonious frontage of the harbourside buildings is thanks to one of the city's most prominent citizens – Francisco Gomes de Avelar, Bishop of Faro in the late 18th century – under whose instructions much of the town was rebuilt after the earthquake of 1755.

Return to the Jardim Manuel Bivar and enter the old town by the Arco da Vila.

5 Largo da Sé

Elegant Rua do Município climbs to the picturesque Largo da Sé, dominated by the cathedral (*open: Mon–Sat 10am–5.30pm, only during services on Sun*) and the Paço Episcopal (Bishop's Palace). Follow the narrow streets to the statue of Afonso III guarding the Museu Municipal de Faro (*see p62*).

Leave the old town via the restored Arco de Repouso, where you can see a bronze casting of the city's Moorish charter. To the right is the vast Largo de São Francisco and its church. Turn left along Rua José Bandeiro.

6 Rua José Bandeiro

Beneath the walls, a low plaque of *azulejos* depicts the Tomada de Faro – the reconquest of the city from the Moors by the Christians in 1249. On the corner behind stands a remarkable Art Nouveau-styled decorative building.

Continue along Rua Manuel Belmarco to join Rua de Santo António, the main shopping street, which leads back to Praça da Liberdade.

Nesting birds on the bell tower of the Arco da Vila

Open: Mon–Fri 10am–1.30pm &
2.30–6pm.

Museu Marítimo (Maritime Museum)

Faro's Maritime Museum, located on
the seafront side of the harbour, houses
a collection of model ships, nautical
gear and a fascinating display of fishing
equipment: tuna harpoons, cuttlefish
traps, spider crab cages and many more
methods for luring creatures from
lagoon and sea.
*Rua Capitania do Porto. Tel: 289 894990.
Open: Mon–Fri 9am–noon & 2.30–5pm.
Admission charge.*

Museu Municipal de Faro
(Faro Municipal Museum)

Once the Prince Henry Archaeological
Museum, this fine Renaissance
building is now home to Faro's
historical museum as well. It is located
in the quiet two-tiered cloister of the
former convent of Nossa Senhora
da Assunção. The façade stands on
the Praça Afonso III, next to the
cathedral square.

Archaeological exhibits on the
ground floor range from prehistoric to
neoclassical, the star attraction being a
large 3rd-century AD Roman mosaic of
Neptune, which was dug up near the
railway station. On the upper gallery of
the cloister, the views of the gargoyles
are more inspiring than the paintings
and pottery on display.
*14 Praça Afonso III. Tel: 289 897400.
Open: Jun–Sept Tue–Fri 10am–7pm,
Sat & Sun 11.30am–6pm; Oct–May*

NEARBY BEACHES

One of the least crowded beaches is Falésia,
which stretches for several kilometres
to the west of Vilamoura. Despite some
development on the cliffs above, you
can always find stretches of near-deserted
sand. Beyond a promontory at the west
end, the Olhos de Água is a small beach
surrounded by cliffs.

The fishing community here is still very
much in evidence, but so are the tourists,
some of them spilling over from Albufeira.

---

*Tue–Fri 10am–6pm, Sat & Sun
10.30am–5pm. Last entry half an
hour before closing.
Admission charge.*

Sé (Cathedral)

On the main square of the old town,
Faro's cathedral is a much-restored
medley of Gothic, Renaissance and
Baroque. Of the original church built in
1251, probably on the site of a former
Moorish mosque, only the tower and
portal survived the 1755 earthquake.
The interior is cool, spacious and
relatively unadorned. The most
impressive features are the 18th-century
glazed tiles in the side chapels.
*Largo da Sé. Open: Mon–Fri 10am–6pm,
Sat 10am–1pm; only during services on
Sun. Admission charge.*

*Faro is on the N125, 305km (190 miles)
southeast of Lisbon and 53km (33 miles)
west of Vila Real de Santo António.
Tourist office: 8 Rua da Misericórdia,
by the Arco da Vila. Tel: 289 803604.
Open: summer daily 9.30am–7pm;*

The old quarter of Vilamoura

*winter Fri–Mon 9.30am–1pm,
2–5.30pm, Tue–Thur 9.30am–5.30pm.*

Vilamoura

Said to be the biggest holiday development in Europe, Vilamoura is an entirely purpose-built resort, covering more than 1,600ha (3,954 acres) of coastal plain. There is no real centre and no real Portuguese charm. What it does offer is a great range of accommodation and a choice of sporting and leisure facilities.

Centred around the marina are multi-storey apartments and luxury four- and five-star hotels, complete with private whirlpools and heated pools. Further out, and stretching for several kilometres, are the ever-expanding clusters of new property complexes, somewhat misleadingly called 'villages'. These are made up of villas, apartments and sports facilities. Some of the most luxurious villas, kitted out with stereo, satellite TV and air conditioning, are set among pine trees beside a golf course. Despite the gargantuan proportions of the resort, construction seems to be never-ending.

The other target is self-sufficiency. Vilamoura already has its own herd of cattle.

What to see and do

If there is a centre to Vilamoura it is the 1,000-berth marina. The largest in southern Europe, this is a showcase for floating palaces, ritzy yachts and ocean-going clippers. There are yacht trips along the coast or fishing excursions for big game.

The older and slightly more attractive quarter of Vilamoura focuses on the beach. Behind, on the main esplanade, waiters vie to draw tourists in to their restaurants. Food in Vilamoura ranges from Chinese takeaway to lobster *cataplana* (casserole).

Vilamoura may be man-made but it is not without a history. The ancient remains across the road from the marina are evidence that there were Roman, Visigothic and Moorish settlements here. Excavations have revealed the foundations of a Roman patrician's house from the 1st century BC and the remnants of fine mosaics. A small **museum** nearby contains all the finds from this site, including Roman lamps and Visigothic coins, as well as depictions of the villa in its prime (*tel: 289 312153. Open: Jun–Sept daily 10am–1pm, 4–9pm; Oct–May daily 9.30am–12.30pm & 2–6pm. Admission charge*).

The evening activities focus on restaurants, bars and the casino. Here you can try your hand at roulette, blackjack, French bank or poker. Added attractions are nightly live shows and a restaurant within the casino (*tel: 289 310000. Open: daily 7pm–1am. Admission charge to the gaming room. Take your passport*).

For sports enthusiasts, Vilamoura has the best choice in the Algarve. There are no fewer than five 18-hole golf courses, spaced around the outskirts of the resort (*see pp150–52*). The favourite is the Old Course, laid out over gently sloping hills with tree-lined fairways. Among other sports, you can try tennis, riding, sailing, windsurfing, waterskiing and scuba diving. Clubs offer lawn bowling, clay-pigeon shooting, badminton and

aerobics. Vilamoura is also the venue for some big sporting events, including sailing regattas and parachuting championships.

Vilamoura is 26km (16 miles) northwest of Faro. Tourist office: in Quarteira, 4km (2¹/₂ miles) away (see below).

Quarteira

Quarteira is often cited as the ugly duckling of the Algarve and it is not difficult to see why. The former fishing village has been swallowed up by a joyless sprawl of tower blocks. The saving grace is the long sandy beach, but even this has its drawbacks, with the hotels right behind and the occasional concrete mixer encroaching on the sands. Despite this, it is still a popular resort,

Vilamoura's fine marina

particularly among people from Lisbon who like to rent or buy new apartments here. One consequence is that bullfights take place in Quarteira's bullring every week during the summer.

On the road to Albufeira, 7km (4 miles) from Quarteira, the **Parque Atlantico** has slides and rides and, in high season, shows are put on by an Acapulco high-diving team.
Parque Atlantico, on the N125.
Tel: 289 397282. Open: summer daily
9.30am–7pm. Closed in winter.
Admission charge.

Quarteira is 22km (14 miles) northwest of Faro, 26km (16 miles) east of Albufeira. Tourist office: Praça do Mar. Tel: 289 389209. Open: Mon–Thur 9.30am–8pm, Fri–Sun & off-season 9.30am–12.30pm & 2–5.30pm.

Vale do Lobo

Vale do Lobo – literally 'Valley of the Wolf' – could hardly be less aptly named. Far from the image of a lean, hungry beast howling in the moonlight, this is an enormous, purpose-built holiday estate of over 750 luxury villas and many more in the pipeline.

Within the low-rise, upmarket complex there are two golf courses, the Roger Taylor Tennis Centre (where amateurs from all over Europe come to have their games reconstructed in intensive tennis courses), numerous other sporting facilities, banks, boutiques, beauty salons, a spa, fitness centre and restaurants and discos galore.

Hundreds of water sprinklers keep the resort's grounds as green and manicured as an English croquet lawn, while gardeners tend exotic shrubs, silent beneath their straw hats. The well-heeled tourists who strut about in the trendiest of leisurewear serve as a reminder of what the whole of the Algarve could have been like if the policy of developing it as a premium holiday destination had not been abandoned in the 1970s.

There is no village of Vale do Lobo other than the tourist resort, which was originally developed in the late 1960s on farmland. Ironically, however, there is far more Algarvian character here than in the nearby resorts of Quarteira, Albufeira and Armação de Pêra, with their high-rise apartment blocks and fish 'n' chip shops.

The highly civilised whitewashed villas of Vale do Lobo are all in the traditional Moorish style, with arched windows and doorways, lattice-work balconies, and low, rounded chimneys topped with tiles.

Vale do Lobo suits holidaymakers looking for stylish, ritzy relaxation – especially people who want to throw in a bit of sport. If you want to enjoy the sand and sea, however, there is no alternative but to forsake this elite paradise for the public beach.
Vale do Lobo is 15km (9 miles) northwest of Faro off the N125.

Almancil

Patterned chimneys and pottery are the main features of the small, unassuming town of Almancil. But, lying by the frenzied N125 highway, it is not a place to linger long.

Quinta do Lago

Just 6km (4 miles) south of Almancil is the Quinta do Lago complex where from dawn to dusk 1,500 sprinklers keep the Algarve's most famous golf course looking lush. The upmarket complex covers 640ha (1,581 acres), with luxury villas dotted among pinewoods and lakes. The Praia do Ançao is a superb, and surprisingly uncrowded, beach.

São Lourenço

What most tourists come to see is the stunningly beautiful little **church** in the nearby village of São Lourenço. Sitting on a hillock east of Almancil, the church and its splendid tiled interior provide an oasis of peace and a feast for the eyes.

Apart from the sumptuous gilded altar, the entire church, including the vaulted ceiling, is embellished with blue and white glazed tiles – or *azulejos* – showing the life of St Lawrence. The tiles are dated 1730 and signed by Policarpo de Oliveira Bernardes who, together with his more famous father, António, established a large workshop and produced tiles that can be found throughout Portugal. In true Algarvian style there is no information available at the church but you might find an old lady outside selling postcards off a table, who can also provide bits of useful and interesting information. Also worth a visit is the local **Centro Cultural**, below the church. This stylish art gallery exhibits works by Portuguese and foreign artists.

The plain exterior of the São Lourenço church gives no hint of its sumptuous interior

The ramparts of Loulé castle offer sweeping views of the surrounding area

Church of São Lourenço: 2km (1¹/₄ miles) east of Almancil, off the N125. Open: Mon–Fri 10am–1.30pm & 2.30–5.30pm, Sat 10am–1.30pm, Sun 2.30–5.30pm. Admission charge. Cultural Centre tel: 289 395475. Open: Tue–Sun noon–7pm.

Almancil is on the N125, 13km (8 miles) northwest of Faro and 7km (4 miles) south of Loulé.

Loulé

Located northwest of Faro, set among orchards of fig, olive and orange trees, Loulé is one of the principal market towns of the Algarve. In a province where the artisan is becoming a dying breed, the town is one of the few genuine handicraft centres. Wander down back alleys north of

the market and you can still hear the hammers of the coppersmiths beating pots and pans in small dim workshops.

To see Loulé at its best, go on a Saturday morning, when colourful market stalls spill into the streets around the mock-Moorish market building. Locals take their pick from the fish and vegetable stalls, while tourists are lured by the cheap, chunky pottery and the handmade hats and baskets. Outside, street stalls are stacked with local produce: bags of almonds, buckets of olives, bunches of herbs, crates of oranges, and sausages in all shapes and sizes.

In the narrow cobbled streets of the centre, the Moorish origins of Loulé are still apparent. Modern shops may be

(*Cont. on p70*)

Tour: São Brás to Estói

This circular motor tour takes in a clutch of churches, the Roman ruins at Milreu and the remarkable rococo palace at Estói. The tour is 34km (21 miles) long and the suggested extension east will add 28km (17 miles). Note that the main sites on this tour are closed on Mondays.

Allow 3 hours.

Start in São Brás de Alportel, 17km (11 miles) north of Faro.

1 São Brás de Alportel

São Brás de Alportel lies well away from the usual tourist circuits in the Barrocal, the limestone zone that lies between the coast and the inland mountains. It has an interesting ethnographic museum. The large parish church, in the square called Largo da Igreja, has an elegant classical façade and bell tower, while the pavement in front is flagged with tombstones. Inside, see the gilded and carved chapel of Senhor dos Passos and paintings of Saints Jerome, Ambrose and Augustine.
Leave Largo da Igreja, with views south towards the Serra de Monte Figo, taking Rua Gago Coutinho to the Largo São Sebastião.

2 Largo São Sebastião

The bust in the small gardens in this square is of Bernardo Ramos, the Portuguese poet.
Turn left on to Rua Luís Bivar and continue 13km (8 miles) to Loulé on the N270.

3 Loulé

The large Gothic parish church stands on the Largo da Matriz, protected on two sides by remains of the town's Moorish walls. A smaller section of fortifications near the Largo Dom Pedro I has been incorporated into the excellent small museum opposite the church of Nossa Senhora da Conceição which, like the parish church, is lined with 17th-century *azulejos* (*see p71*).
Leave Loulé via the Avenida Marçal Pacheco (towards Faro). After 5km (3 miles), at Valados, take the turning for Santa Bárbara de Nexe, just before the intersection with the motorway.

4 Santa Bárbara de Nexe

The bell tower of the 15th-century parish church rises above the roofs of the village. Inside is a Manueline-style arch, an early 18th-century tile panel depicting St Barbara, and a tiled sacristy.
Take the Faro road and then turn left at Falfosa on to the 520-2 to Estói. At the crossroads with the N2, go straight on.

5 Ruinas de Milreu

Before the village of Estói, the ruins of Milreu (*open: Tue–Sun 9.30am–12.30pm & 2–5pm. Admission charge*) lie just off the road on the left. First excavated in 1877, this Roman villa and bath complex was probably connected to the nearby port of Ossonoba (modern Faro). The remains include a bath, later used as a Christian church, and mosaics depicting fish. The small museum is excellent.

Continue to Estói, parking near the parish church of São Martinho, which is much older than its 19th-century façade. At the end of the street, to the left, a pair of ornamental wrought-iron gates leads to one of the Algarve's most astonishing sights, the Palácio de Estói.

6 Palácio de Estói

The palace, a lavish rococo structure built in the late 18th century, is now a *pousada* (state-run) hotel. The historic mansion, which once belonged to the Dukes of Estói, has beautiful gardens, currently under restoration, with balustrade terraces and a double staircase concealing a grotto with a replica of Canova's *Three Graces*.

You can take the N2 from Estói to return to São Brás. Alternatively, follow the Monte Figo hills east, along the N516, to Moncarapacho, a village with two churches of interest and limestone caves (grutas) nearby. Then take the N398 north and then the N270 west (near another cave, the Gruta dos Arrifes) to return to São Brás de Alportel.

Tour: São Brás to Estói

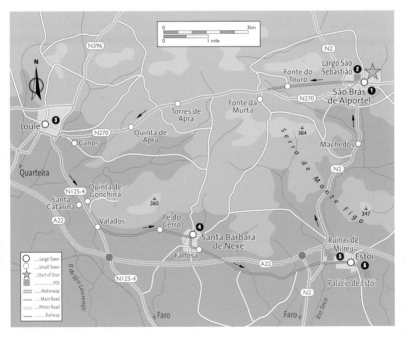

taking over from artisans' workshops but many of them still specialise in the local handicrafts, such as baskets made from *esparto* grass, mule saddles, ironwork, leather goods, woodcarvings, lacemaking and earthenware vessels.

The big event of the year in Loulé is the carnival. Crowds come from all over the Algarve to watch the colourful floats, the marching bands and the Battle of Flowers. The main religious procession is held two weeks after Easter when a statue of the town's patron saint, Our Lady of Sorrows, is taken back to her sanctuary in the 16th-century chapel (of the same name) which is set on a hill just to the west of Loulé.

Castelo (Castle)

Of Arab origin, Loulé's castle has been in Portuguese hands since 1249 when the remaining Moorish parts of the Algarve were reconquered. Little remains of the castle itself, but the restored walls and towers afford panoramic views of Loulé and the surrounding landscape. There is a small archaeological museum with Roman and later finds from the region.
Rua Paio Perez Correia. Tel: 289 400642. Open: Mon–Fri 9am–5.30pm, Sat 9am–1pm. Admission charge to museum.

Igreja Matriz (Parish Church)

The handsome Gothic parish church is easily distinguished by its lofty onion-domed bell tower, converted from the minaret of the mosque on whose foundations the church is built. Inside there are some beautifully tiled chapels, notably the first on the right, depicting the Nativity, and the first on the left, depicting the Adoration of the Magi.

The second chapel on the left has typically Manueline carvings. In contrast to many Portuguese churches of that age, the interior is relatively plain, focusing attention on the side altars and on the ornate 18th-century gilded woodcarving and statues of the main altar.

The church stands on a square overlooking the charming, but oddly named, Jardim dos Amuados, or Sulky People's Garden.
Largo da Matriz. Open: Tue–Fri 9–11am, Sat 9am–7pm.

PORTUGUESE WATER DOGS

From an ancient herding breed, the Portuguese Water Dog was developed by early fishing societies, who taught these naturally good swimmers (they have webbed toes) to herd schools of fish and retrieve nets. So valued were these appealing curly-haired dogs that they were regarded as crew members, complete with their share of the catch as food. Numbers diminished with the modernisation of methods, and the breed was endangered until it was internationally recognised in the 1930s. Still rare, they are occasionally seen in the Algarve (you might mistake them for untrimmed black poodles). A kennel at the Parque Natural da Ria Formosa, near Olhão, offers a chance to meet and learn about them.

**Igreja de Nossa Senhora
da Conceição
(Church of Our Lady of the
Immaculate Conception)**

Close to the castle, this small church
looks very simple from the exterior,
but it has an elaborate carved gold-
washed altarpiece and walls that are
almost entirely covered with 18th-
century blue and white *azulejos*. The
biblical scenes depicted include the
Presentation of the Virgin at the
Temple, the Circumcision of Christ
and the Adoration of the Magi.
Rua Paio Perez Correia.
Open: Tue, Thur & Sat 9am–1pm.

*Loulé is 18km (11 miles) northwest of Faro.
Tourist office: Avenida 25 de Abril 9. Tel:
289 463900. Open: Mon–Fri 9.30am–7pm
(5.30pm in winter), Sat, Sun & off-season
weekdays 9.30am–1pm & 2–5.30pm.*

Olhão

The old quarter of Olhão, with its
cube-shaped, flat-roofed houses and
stepped terraces, looks remarkably like
an African *kasbah*, and you could be
forgiven for thinking that the Moors
had left their mark here in ancient
times. In fact, Olhão was only
developed in the early 19th century; it
(Cont. on p74)

The popular municipal market at Olhão

Tour: Castles and caves around Loulé

This 62km (39-mile) tour takes in some of the Algarve's more ancient landmarks – both natural (the waterfall at Alte and the caves of Rocha da Pena and Rocha dos Soidos) and man-made (the Moorish castles of Salir and Paderne).

Allow 4 hours.

From Loulé, take the Salir road through Assumada. After 7km (4 miles), you will cross the Algibre River at the Roman bridge – the Ponte de Tor. Here you can detour right to follow the Fonte de Benémola walk (see pp82–3). Otherwise, continue on to Salir.

1 Salir

Until the reconquest by Afonso III in 1248, Salir was a Moorish stronghold with a mighty castle. As early as the 16th century, the fortress was in ruins and the present village was built over the Muslim settlement. The remaining walls stand to the west of the church; follow signs to the castle, parking below in the tree-lined lane to the left and walking up the hill, where the narrow streets are for residents' vehicles only. Much of the walls was built of *taipa*, a mixture of clay, sand, straw and water, typical of the Almóada period of Moorish architecture.

There are superb views of the countryside from the church, and if it is open, you can look inside to see the illuminated 1550 Papal Bull signed by Pope Paul III.

From Salir, follow the N124 west towards Alte. After 4km (2¹/₂ miles), turn right at Pena de Baixo and continue for 1km (²/₃ mile) to Rocha.

2 Rocha

The Rocha da Pena, at 479m (1,572ft), is an ancient outcrop of the Serra do Caldeirão mountain range, which lies to the northwest and has remains of Moorish, Roman and even Neolithic occupation.

From the village of Rocha, a footpath leads round the outcrop, returning alongside a group of windmills. If you wish, you can drive east of Alte to the Rocha dos Soidos, or explore on foot. Both hills have deep caves, or *grutas*.

If you do not follow the diversion, return to the N124 and continue west to Alte via Benafim Grande, which has a monthly market every first Saturday and an annual fair in late October.

3 Alte

Alte (*see p55*) is regarded as the prettiest of the Algarve villages. You can explore the nearby *fontes* or springs, the tiled, vaulted parish church, the São Luís chapel and the Queda do Vigario waterfall – as well as several cafés and restaurants. The Fonte Grande is the backdrop both to the May Day Festival and to the Folklore Festival on the second Sunday in August.

Leave Alte by the N124 Salir road, then turn right on to the EM1354 to Paderne via Brito and Lentiscais.

4 Paderne

Paderne is another ancient village with a Moorish heritage. Follow the road to Fonte de Paderne, southwest of the village, and continue along a track with the castle ahead. Below the castle, a steep path leads down into the valley and across to the opposite hill via an ancient and remote Roman bridge. In Paderne itself, see the 16th-century parish church, which was rebuilt after the 1755 earthquake, the Nossa Senhora do Pé chapel, and the remains of the 12th-century Arab castle.

If you collect unusual place names, you may like to make a 1km (²/₃-mile) detour west of Paderne to the hamlet of Purgatório. Otherwise, head south to Boliqueime, where Grogan's British Pub is a favourite hangout for British visitors. To go back to Loulé, take the N125 east and then the N270.

Tour: Castles and caves around Loulé

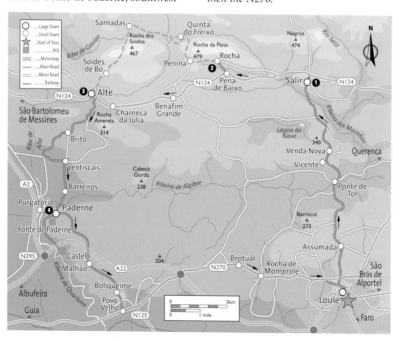

A lone black-winged stilt in the Parque Natural da Ria Formosa

was through commercial links with North Africa that the town developed this Arabic style of architecture.

Olhão was put on the map by a group of intrepid fishermen. In 1808, they sailed in a small boat across the Atlantic to Rio de Janeiro where they informed the exiled Portuguese monarch, King João VI, that Napoleon's troops had been driven from his kingdom. As a reward the seashore village was raised to the status of a town and called Olhão da Restauração (Olhão of the Restoration). The fishing community expanded, canneries were established, and by the late 19th century Olhão had become a busy port.

Olhão is still a major port today. It is not immediately appealing because of its sprawling modern outskirts, but the old fishermen's quarters, the fish market and the restaurants (serving some of the freshest fish in the Algarve) make it well worth a visit.

The two offshore islands, both part of the Parque Natural da Ria Formosa and linked to Olhão by ferry, are fringed with sandy beaches.

Fish market

The fish and food markets are housed in distinctive red-brick turreted buildings on the seafront. The variety of fish and seafood sold here is amazing, from the humble sardine – taken away in bagfuls by local housewives – to the luxury lobster, which is whisked off by local restaurateurs as soon as the markets are open.

Avenida 5 de Outubro. Open: Mon–Sat 7am–1pm. Closed: Sun.

Igreja de Nossa Senhora do Rosário (Church of Our Lady of the Rosary)

This large, late 17th-century Baroque church was built with donations from local fishermen. The main reason for a visit is the bird's-eye view from the

NEARBY

The pretty village of Moncarapacho lies 7km (4 miles) northwest of Olhão. The parish church has a finely carved Renaissance portal and, close by, the chapel of Santo Cristo is covered with decorative 18th-century *azulejos*. The adjoining museum has an idiosyncratic collection of archaeological finds and sacred art.

belfry over the town's rooftops, chimneys and TV aerials. Beware of the booming bells that chime on the hour.

To the rear of the church is a tiny open chapel, dedicated to Nossa Senhora dos Aflitos (Our Lady of the Suffering), where candles burn among wax *ex votos* of human legs, arms and faces. For years, the wives of Olhão's fishermen have been coming here to pray for their men at sea.
Praça da Restauração. Open: 9am–noon & 4.30–5.30pm. Closed: Mon. For access to the belfry, ask in the sacristy.

Ilha da Armona and Ilha da Culatra

From June to September, ferries run roughly every 1½ hours to Olhão's two offshore islands. The Ilha da Armona takes 15 minutes by ferry. The service is less frequent during the rest of the year. For the best beach, you need to walk about 1km (²/₃ mile), to the far side of the island. On the Ilha da Culatra, get off the ferry at the second stop, Furol, where there are sandy beaches.
Olhão is 9km (6 miles) east of Faro. Tourist office: Largo Sebastião Martins Mestre. Tel: 289 713936. Open: daily 9.30am–12.30pm & 2.30–7pm (5.30pm off-season).

Tavira

The town of Tavira, not far from the frontier with Spain, has an elegance rarely found in the Algarve. Straddling the Gilão River (which upstream becomes the Ségua), it is a town with handsome 18th-century houses and a

Elegant Tavira beside the Gilão River

Eastern Algarve

NEARBY BEACHES

The best beaches are on the Ilha de Tavira, stretching for 11km (7 miles). Buses link the centre of Tavira with the ferry landing stage about 2km (1¼ miles) away. Ferries land at the eastern tip of the island which, at this point, is crowded and unappealing – for a decent stretch of beach you must walk further along the shore.

skyline pierced by castle ramparts, plus the domes and spires of over 35 churches. Compared with towns west of Faro, there is a refreshing absence of unsightly development.

History

Formerly an Arab settlement, Tavira was conquered in 1242 by Dom Paio Peres Correia in revenge for the death of seven Christian knights who were killed by the Moors, during a truce, while they were out hunting near the town. Tavira later became a major port, but the plague of 1645 drastically reduced its population. Subsequent earthquake damage and the silting up of the port led to its economic decline.

For centuries, Tavira's mainstay was tuna fishing. Until the 1970s, by which time stocks were severely depleted, tuna were trapped in nets, killed by a team of harpooners and hoisted aboard the boats. These bloody battles between tuna fish and harpooners were aptly described as 'bullfights of the sea'.

Tavira today

Tavira still has a prosperous air and retains some of its fine classical façades.

On the south side of the river, gardens with palms run alongside the water as far as the Mercado da Riberia, the former covered market. This is now a centre for shops, cafés and occasional

Riverside park in Tavira

exhibitions by local artists. The far end of the market is given over to fish and seafood, much of it bought by the fish restaurants by the quayside. The new market lies behind the Hotel Vila Galé and here you can find stalls selling oranges and lemons, almonds, olives and figs, all from the fertile farmlands of the Sotavento (the leeward coast of the Algarve, stretching from Faro to the Spanish border).

Upstream, the arched stone bridge has Roman foundations. A plaque on the south side commemorates the bravery of the locals when they repelled the invading troops of King Juan I of Castile between 1383 and 1385.

Castelo dos Muros (Castle)
The castle is reached by means of a cobbled alley that leads up from the main square, the Praça da República. All that remains of the castle are the walls, but from the neighbouring gardens there are good views of the river and of Tavira's rooftops and churches. The latest lookout point is the **Torre de Tavira**, an old water tower. A lift takes you to the top for fascinating camera obscura views of real-time Tavira – all done with mirrors.
Open: daily 9am–5pm. Free admission to castle; admission charge for Torre de Tavira.

Igreja da Misericórdia (Church of Mercy)
From the outside, you can admire the very finely carved Renaissance portal

dating from the 1540s. The interior has fine *azulejos* and gilded woodwork.
Rua da Galeria. Open: Mon–Fri 9.30am–12.30pm. Free admission.

Igreja de Santa Maria do Castelo (Church of Santa Maria of the Castle)
This simple whitewashed church, beside the castle ramparts, stands on the ruins of a former mosque. It was built in the 13th century but reconstructed after the 1755 earthquake. The church contains the tombs of Dom Paio Peres Correia and the Sete Caçadores, the seven Christian knights massacred by the Moors, thus precipitating the reconquest of the town.
Open: Mon–Fri 2–6.30pm.

Tavira is 30km (19 miles) northeast of Faro and 23km (14 miles) west of the Spanish border. Tourist office: Rua da Galeria 9 (off Praça da República). Tel: 281 322511. Open: daily 9.30am–7pm (until 5.30pm in winter).

Monte Gordo
Close to the Spanish border, Monte Gordo is the resort that smacks most of the Spanish *costas*. Concrete blocks predominate and the centre has none of the fishing-village charm so typical of the majority of the Algarve resorts. Now that Spain is linked to the Algarve by a bridge across the Guadiana River, the number of visitors has increased and development has been substantial.

On the plus side, Monte Gordo has a huge beach with pale golden sand and the warmest waters along the Algarve

Eastern Algarve

Vila Real de Santo António

coastline. The boulevard running parallel to the beach provides a variety of eating places, from burger bars to restaurants serving clam *cataplana* (casserole). Large hotels and apartment blocks loom behind the beach, with a hinterland of sandy pinewoods providing some relief. Nightlife centres either around the casino, which is right on the beach, or in discos and late-night bars.

Monte Gordo is 5km (3 miles) west of Vila Real de Santo António, 52km (32 miles) east of Faro, close to the Spanish border. Tourist office: Rua Infante Dom Henrique. Tel: 281 544495. Open: daily 9.30am–7pm in summer, 9.30am–1pm & 2–5.30pm off-season.

Vila Real de Santo António

Washed away by the waves in the 17th century, Vila Real de Santo António rose again like a phoenix in 1774. It took just five months to rebuild, due largely to the ingenuity of the Marquês de Pombal, Chief Minister to King José. The town was constructed as a model fishing port, designed with the same grid pattern of streets and uniform façades as the Baixa quarter of Lisbon, which Pombal had reconstructed after the 1755 earthquake.

Today, Vila Real is best known as the principal border town between the Algarve and Spain. Located on the western shores of the Guadiana River, it faces the small Spanish town of Ayamonte across the water. Just 6km (4 miles) upstream, a handsome bridge spans the Guadiana, creating a road link with Spain and increasing the flow of traffic into southern Portugal.

The 18th-century houses in the centre give the town a certain elegance, though this is partially spoilt by an overabundance of souvenir and T-shirt shops catering for Spanish day-trippers. Although tourism has taken over from fishing as the main money-spinner, tuna fish are still processed here, and local fishermen supply their catch to the morning market.

Still in the centre, the Praça do Marquês de Pombal is a handsome square, paved black and white and bordered by well-proportioned 18th-century houses. On the river, ferries ply to and from Spain, patrol boats snoop around the waters, and wading birds nose in the mud.

The ferry crossing is cheap and fun, but Ayamonte itself is no more than a very ordinary border town. The ferry service operates every half-hour (*from 8/8.30am until 11pm in summer; or to 7.30pm in winter*). Day-cruiser trips along the scenic Guadiana River operate twice a week (*tel: 281 422220*). *Vila Real de Santo António is 53km (33 miles) northeast of Faro, on the border with Spain. Tourist office: Centro Cultural, Rua Teófilo Braga. Tel: 281 542100. Open: daily 9.30am–1pm & 2.30–5pm.*

Castro Marim

Rising from the marshlands west of the Guadiana River, the hill town of Castro Marim enjoys a bird's-eye view of southern Spain. The town and its castle occupy a strategic position, protecting the southern Portuguese coast. The Phoenicians based themselves here while mining for copper and tin; the Moors then settled for several centuries until the Christians ejected them in 1242.

In 1319, the town became the headquarters of the Order of Christ. This newly formed military/religious order played an instrumental role in the voyages that marked the beginning of the Age of Discovery. Prince Henry the Navigator was appointed governor of the order and, if the inscription inside the castle entrance is to be believed, he was once a resident here.

Set within massive walls, the main hilltop **castle** of Castro Marim dominates the town and was built by King Afonso III in the 13th century. It

Castro Marim's main church

was destroyed by the 1755 earthquake, but the battlemented walls and a ruined church still survive.

There is also a small museum in the castle which provides an overview of Castro Marim, past and present. Exhibits include spearheads, cannon-balls, hunting traps, farming tools, and explanations of the surrounding salt pans and nature reserve. Walk the battlements for a splendid panorama of the surrounding countryside.

The fortress of São Sebastião, built four centuries after the castle (and currently under restoration), can be seen sitting on a hillock to the southwest. To the east lies the Spanish border town of Ayamonte, while to the south is the Portuguese border town of Vila Real de Santo António.

Spread out below are the flat salt pans of the Reserva do Sapal nature reserve. Keep your eyes peeled for storks and black-winged stilts. Ask at the castle for a map of the reserve. *Castle. Open: daily 9am–7pm, 5pm off-season. Castro Marim is on the N122,* *4km (2½ miles) northwest of Vila Real de Santo António. Tourist office: Rua José Alves Moreira 2/4. Tel: 281 531232. Open: Mon–Fri 9.30am–1pm & 2–5.30pm.*

Alcoutim

Only the placid waters of the Guadiana River divide Alcoutim from its former Spanish rival, Sanlúcar de Guadiana. So close are these riverside villages that you can sometimes spot the storks nesting in the Spanish belfries on the other bank.

Originally a fortified stronghold and strategic river port, Alcoutim has, in recent centuries, been no more than a sleepy waterside village, with fishing and handicrafts as its main activities. Far removed from the frenzy of the coast, it still attracts only a sprinkling of visitors.

Above the centre of the village, a 14th-century castle and small archaeological museum stand on a hillock; from here you have a bird's-eye view of Portuguese and Spanish fishing

The Moorish fort at Castro Marim

smacks and swish foreign yachts. The other sights of Alcoutim are the parish church, by the river, with a Renaissance portal, and the church of Nossa Senhora da Conceição, at the top of the village, with a Manueline portal and 18th-century altarpiece.

The loveliest drive in this region follows the banks of the Guadiana for about 19km (12 miles) downstream to Foz de Odeleite, joining the main N122 between Odeleite and Azinhal. From the riverbank, you glimpse the quiet hills of southern Spain, while on the Portuguese side lies the occasional riverside hamlet where locals till the lush land or tend to small patches of vines and vegetables. Day and evening river cruises depart from the ferry pier at Vila Real de Santo António, anchoring at Foz de Odeleite for a lunch or dinner break before heading on to Alcoutim. (*For information, visit www.riosultravel.com. Tel: 281 510200.*)

Alcoutim is on the N122, 44km (27 miles) north of Vila Real de Santo António. Tourist office: Rua 1° de Maio. Tel: 281 546179. Open: May–Sept Tue–Thur 9.30am–7pm, Fri–Mon 9.30am–1pm & 2–5.30pm; Oct–Apr Tue–Thur 9.30am–5.30pm, Fri–Mon 9.30am–1pm & 2–5.30pm.

West of Alcoutim

A drive through the rolling hills west of Alcoutim, and a detour to one or two of the isolated villages, will give you a real taste of one of the most remote

Alcoutim sits under its castle

regions of the Algarve. Look out en route for specialist crafts of the region: these include pottery, basketry, blankets, and rugs made to centuries-old designs.

Parque Mineiro Cova dos Mouros (Cova dos Mouros Mine Park)

In the remote hills southwest of Alcoutim, vestiges of a Copper Age mining settlement can be seen at the Parque Mineiro Cova dos Mouros. A 1km (²/₃-mile) walk takes you past old mine shafts, furnaces and reconstructions of primitive dwellings. For youngsters there are donkey rides, gold prospecting and the simulation of an archaeological excavation.

The Parque Mineiro Cova dos Mouros is 2km (1¼ miles) south of Vaqueiros. Tel: 289 999299. http://minacovamouros.sitepac.pt. Tours by reservation only. Admission charge.

Walk: To the Fonte de Benémola

The hills north of Loulé are a world away from the villas of 'tourist Algarve'; they are riddled with caves and springs, and ancient villages lie in the valleys between. Querença and its sister village, Aldeia da Tor, date back to Roman times and are separated by the fertile valley of the Ribeira da Fonte Menalva.

Allow 3 hours.

You can follow the valley upstream to the Fonte de Benémola, a spring (fonte) that joins the river at a shallow fording point classified as an area of natural interest, and then return along the opposite bank. The circuit is 4km (2¹/₂ miles), but you can extend it further into the valley and explore the villages themselves, or incorporate the

walk into the motor tour from Loulé (see pp68–9).

Follow the N396 10km (6 miles) north of Loulé, then turn left on to the N524 passing the turning to Querença. The start of the path to the Fonte de Benémola is signposted 3km (2 miles) after the turning to the right, just before a left-hand bend. If you pass the Quinta da Passagem and bridge over the river you have gone too far.

NEARBY VILLAGES

The nearby villages are also worth exploring, especially Querença. The church of Nossa Senhora do Pé da Cruz has a Manueline doorway and, if you find it open, *azulejos* inside. The church at Aldeia da Tor is dedicated to Saint Rita, and the bridge that crosses the Algibre River, to the hamlet of Ponte de Tôr, is Roman.

Even better would be to visit the villages during one of their annual fairs. Aldeia da Tor has a wine festival on 16 January, while Querença's Festa das Chouriças – celebrating the local smoked sausage – also takes place in late January. There are more festivities at Easter, on 24 June for the festival of São João (St John), and again on 15 August, the Feast of Nossa Senhora da Assunção (the Assumption).

The walk starts in an area known as the Vale de Mulher. The fertile floodplain along the banks is divided into cultivated smallholdings. Water is brought to the fields by waterwheels (*noras* in Portuguese) located at the side of the stream.

After walking for just over 1km (²/₃ mile), you will pass a path that branches off to the right to another group of cottages. Keep on the main track which bears left and crosses a tributary of the main stream, the Ribeira da Chapa.

The path returns towards the main stream again (ignore another path off to the right) and soon follows alongside the water. After less than 1km (²/₃ mile), you will arrive at the spring – here the stream opens out and is crossed by a rocky ford, passable with care, but beware of mossy stones. The path continues to follow the stream bed (all but dry above here) into the valley, but a section of large boulders makes the going quite difficult at first. The ravine narrows and can be eerily silent: in the hillside above and to the right are two caves of repute – the cavernous **Gruta da Salustria** and the **Igrejinha dos Mouros** (Church of the Moors), both of which have stalactites and stalagmites.

Return to the ford and cross over to the right bank.

The shady path follows closer to the water on this side, past more small springs. In spring, look out for arum lilies growing alongside the path.

Ignore the paths to the right and, after nearly 2km (1¹/₄ miles), you will pass a group of cork oaks before dropping down to rejoin the road next to the bridge. Turn left and walk a short way back along the N524 to your car.

Walk: To the Fonte de Benémola

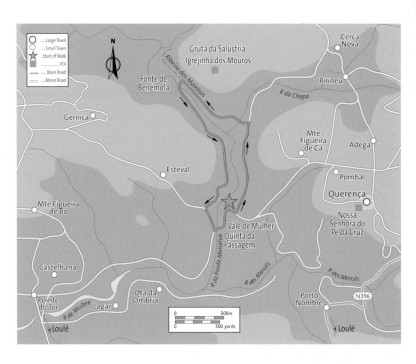

Lower Alentejo

The Alentejo – literally 'beyond the (River) Tejo' – is a vast sun-baked plain; it is bordered, to the east, by a long backbone of craggy hills that form a natural frontier with Spain, and, to the west, by the Atlantic. Southwards are the throbbing tourist resorts of the Algarve, the huge majority of whose visitors never venture more than a few kilometres inland.

Yet, just a couple of hours' drive from the hotel-lined sandy beaches and manicured greens of the Algarve, there is some of the least-explored country in the Iberian peninsula. Gently rolling landscapes of golden grain are dotted by cork oaks, and hillsides of olive groves march in straight rows to the horizon. The northern and southern parts of the Alentejo are somewhat roughly divided by long flooded valleys of the impoundment held by the Barragem de Alqueva dam. Tops of rounded hills stand out as islands. Out of this rolling plain, the towns of Serpa, Moura and Beja rise, two of them encircled by walls, all crowned by castles.

Tourism lies very lightly on the land here. A scattering of *pousadas* has opened, part of a government initiative to help bring travellers into the less visited regions, and they have been followed by a few upmarket villa hotels. A new international airport has been under construction for some time in Beja, but progress is slow and its opening date is mere speculation. The hope is that it will attract international charter carriers.

Don't get the idea that this rural agricultural area is out of touch with the 21st century, however. The world's largest solar photovoltaic farm, where more than 2,500 giant panels track the sun across the sky each day, is already generating electricity near Moura. That small town has the distinction of having Europe's most annual sunshine.

Beja

When the national weather forecast is shown on Portuguese television, Beja almost invariably stands out as having recorded that day's highest temperature. The capital of Baixo (Lower) Alentejo, Beja is at the hub of the region's expansive plains of wheat fields, cork oak forests and olive groves. In spring, you approach the town along roads lined with poppies, with carpets of bluebells beyond; by high summer the land has been

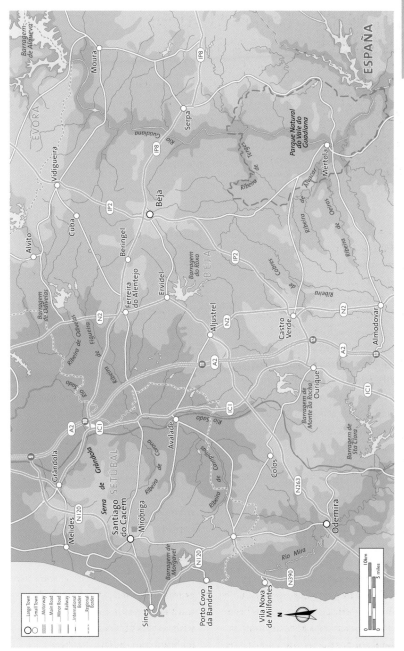

ESPAÑA

Parque Natural
do Vale do
Guadiana

EVORA

Barragem
de Alqueva

Moura

Serpa

Rio Guadiana

Vidigueira

Beja

BEJA

Mértola

Cuba

Alvito

IP2

IP8

IP8

IP2

Beringel

Ervidel

Barragem
do Roxo

Ribeira de Terges

Ribeira de Alyares

Ferreira
do Alentejo

N2

Aljustrel

N2

Castro
Verde

Almodôvar

N2

Ribeira de Cobres

Ribeira de Oeiros

Ribeira

Barragem
de Odivelas

Figueira

Ribeira de Odivelas

Rio Sado

A2

ICl

Ourique

ICl

A2

Barragem
de Monte da Rocha

Barragem de
Sta Clara

Grândola

A2

ICl

Serra de Grândola

SETÚBAL

Avalade

Ribeira de Corona

Ribeira de Campilhas

Rio Sado

Colos

N263

Melides

N120

Santiago
do Cacém

Mirobriga

Barragem de
Morgável

N120

Odemira

Rio Mira

Sines

Porto Covo
da Bandeira

Vila Nova
de Milfontes

N390

N

Large Town
Small Town
Motorway
Main Road
Minor Road
Railway
International
Border
Regional
Border

10km
5 miles

0
0

THE PASSIONATE NUN

The most famous resident of the Nossa Senhora da Conceição convent was Sister Mariana Alcoforado. She had a passionate love affair with a French count who lived in Beja during the war that Portugal fought with Spain between 1661 and 1668.

The erotically pious letters she wrote to him after his departure were, reputedly, published in French in 1669 as *Letters of a Portuguese Nun*. Her cell has a barred window through which she and the count are said to have 'made love'.

scorched into an endless brown. Inhabited since Celtic times, Beja was an important Roman settlement, at the crossroads of two major routes, and has remained so.

Beja is an uncharacteristically busy town whose prosperity is underlined by supermarkets, brimming shops and smart modern buildings. However, anybody who is trying to get under the skin of the region's history and culture should visit Beja, if only to see the Convento da Nossa Senhora da Conceição. Another ruined convent, Convento de São Francisco, has been rebuilt as a 37-bedroom *pousada*.

A lively street market fills the area beneath the castle walls on Saturday mornings, and behind the castle is one of a handful of churches remaining in Portugal that predate the Romanesque era. The Visigothic Santo Amaro, dating from as early as the 6th century, is a fitting home for the city's small archaeological museum, exhibiting some extraordinary examples of very

early stone carving (*admission is included in the ticket for the Regional Museum*).

Castelo (Castle)

There's not much left of the 40 towers that formed the outer walls of this massive fortress, built by King Dinis in the 14th century. But the impressive 40m (131ft) keep is the tallest in Portugal, and the surrounding walls of the central castle are kept in excellent condition. A 180-degree spiral staircase leads to a gallery at the top of the keep, from which there are panoramic views. There is also a small military museum in the courtyard, which is worth a quick look.

Largo do Lidador. Open: Tue–Sun 10am–noon & 2–6pm. Admission charge for tower.

Convento da Nossa Senhora da Conceição (Convent of Our Lady of the Immaculate Conception)

This 15th-century convent is one of the most beautiful buildings in the Alentejo, and an excellent example of the transitional style of architecture between Gothic and Manueline. The convent was among the wealthiest in Portugal and has a fine Sala do Capítulo (chapterhouse) and stone-carved cloisters decorated with some of the finest 15th-century *azulejo* tiles to be found anywhere in Portugal.

The chapel is fronted by a Baroque altarpiece of carved and gilded wood. It also has a wonderful, serene atmosphere and it is well worth your while to pause here for a few minutes, especially if you are lucky enough to have it to yourself.

The Museu Regional (Regional Museum) has a rich collection of artefacts from prehistory to the present day. Exhibits include Roman coins and mosaics found on the site, treasure dating from the convent's wealthy heyday (including a large Ming-dynasty bowl) and works of art from demolished or dismantled churches in the region. An interesting exhibit is the strange tomb built in the shape of a barrel, apparently for a winemaker. There is also a small collection of 16th-century paintings, including the Flemish *Our Lady of the Milk*.

Largo Nossa Senhora da Conceição. Tel: 284 311511. www.museuregionaldebeja.net. Open: Tue–Sun 9.30am–12.30pm & 2–5.15pm. Admission charge.

Beja is on the N260, 27km (17 miles) west of Serpa. Tourist office: 25 Rua do Capitão JF de Sousa. Tel: 284 311913. www.cm-beja.pt. Open: May–Sept Mon–Sat 9am–7pm; Oct–Apr 10am–1pm & 2–6pm.

Moura

Moura means a 'Moorish maiden' and the name refers to the legendary Salúquia, the daughter of a Moorish nobleman from Al-Manija (as the town was then called). Her marriage came to grief when her bridegroom and his entourage were attacked and killed by a band of Christians on their way to the wedding ceremony.

The Christians then donned the nuptial clothes of their victims convincingly enough for the city's drawbridge to be lowered for them. By (*Cont. on p90*)

Lower Alentejo

Convento da Nossa Senhora da Conceição, Beja

Wildlife

Southern Portugal has a varied wildlife, though some animals are under threat. The wolf (*lobo*) could still be found in southern Portugal up until 20 years ago. Both the badger (*texugo*) and the fox (*raposo*) are increasingly rare. Only slightly more common is the civet cat (*gato de Algália*), regarded as a threat to poultry and shot on sight. The rabbit (*coelho*) is hunted for its meat and is more plentiful than the hare (*lebre*), especially in the Barrocal region of the Algarve.

The only venomous snake in the south is the snub-nosed viper, found in the mountains. The one you are most likely to see is the horseshoe snake, which is dark with yellow spots and a mark on its neck that explains its name. There are several types of lizard, including salamanders, chameleons, geckos and the European green lizard. Even greater variety can be found in the region's birdlife, since Portugal is on the main route for migrating birds.

Two major reserves are in the eastern Algarve: the Salt Marsh Natural Reserve at Castro Marim, and the Ria Formosa, which stretches eastwards along the southern coast from Faro to the islands of Tavira. Salt Marsh offers 153 species, among them storks, avocets, flamingos, sandpipers and mallards. These vary with the seasons, since the reserve is home to both nesting and migrating birds. The visitors' centre at Cerro da Rocha is a good place to get

Kestrel

information on various species and suggested sighting points.

The Ria Formosa is renowned for nesting and migrating waterbirds, with over 20,000 regular migrants wintering there. Reed beds and salt pans provide habitat for several nesting species, and the tidal lagoons of Ilha de Tavira, easy for birdwatchers to reach, are habitat for redstart, warblers and several others. Sardinian warblers, golden oriole, waxbills and nightjars are seen regularly. Waders and spoonbillls are a common sight in the Tavira salt pans.

Spring migration between March and May is the time for avid birdwatchers to be in the Alentejo, when the landscapes are also covered in wild flowers and entire meadows are brilliant blue, red or yellow with blossoms. Several bird species winter here, including wood pigeons and golden plover. The Alentejo coast is home to waterbirds, and there is a nature reserve on the Tróia Peninsula.

Golden eagles are now very rare but red kites and kestrels are not unusual. Startling, but common, is the sight of the brightly coloured hoopoe.

Egrets can be found, with many other waders, at the mouth of the Guadiana River, and cattle egrets can be seen in the Alentejo. The eastern Alentejo is home to flocks of azure-winged magpies. Also quite common

White storks can be seen all over the Algarve

in the south is the white stork (*cegonha*), which builds its great nest on church bell towers or other high buildings and on rock crags along the coast.

this means they were able to capture the town, and Salúquia, the Moura, threw herself from the castle tower in grief. The story is unusual among Portuguese folk legends in that it casts the Christians in the role of villains.

More prosaic history books have it that Moura first fell to the Christians in 1165, and that it subsequently changed hands several times. Today, it is a fairly busy agricultural town with a lively Mouraria (Moorish quarter) of stone streets and low houses pierced by arches and ornamented with rounded, tile-topped chimneys. The castle is now a ruin, having been blown up during the Spanish War of Succession, although the keep, a tower and parts of the wall are still there.

The 13th-century Convento do Carmo, the first Carmelite convent in Portugal, is worth a visit to see the frescoed ceiling in the chancel, which was rebuilt in 1725. The Gothic Church de São João is also interesting; notice the stone pulpit supported on a slender column, as well as the fan groining with carved medallions in the chancel. *Azulejo* tile panels from the 17th century decorate the walls here and in the side altars.

Moura is 35km (22 miles) northeast of Serpa at the hub of seven roads radiating out across east-central Alentejo.

Serpa

Serpa stands slightly elevated from the fertile plains of the Alentejo on the first folds of the mountains that form Portugal's eastern border. Low-built whitewashed houses with red-tiled roofs line the streets, while the balconies of grander homes overlook white-paved squares. These days, the town is a fairly important agricultural hub, although, if you turn up on a summer's afternoon, you might be forgiven for suspecting that a Pied Piper had led away the entire population, save the occasional old man whiling away the hours in the shade. Later in the day, when the cottage windows are unshuttered and the cafés open, Serpa can be the place to feel the soul of the Alentejo embodied.

Houses in the old part of the town are dwarfed by remains of the rambling and ruinous fortress, by some formidably sturdy and crenellated stretches of the city wall and by a high slender aqueduct. The **castle** and fortifications were built by King Dinis after the Moors were finally driven out in 1232; most of the damage they sustained occurred nearly 500 years later, during the Spanish War

CAPELA DE SÃO GENS

About 2km (1¼ miles) out of town, next to Serpa's modern *estalagem* (hotel) (which enjoys glorious views over the plains), is a small former mosque, now called the Capela de São Gens. This is one of only two known mosques surviving in Portugal, the other one being at Mértola. It is a quintessentially Moorish building of low domes, archways and finials, all washed glaringly white to reflect the sun. (*Largo do Salvador; take the N260 signposted 'Espanha' eastwards out of Serpa, and turn right following the sign to the estalagem. Open: daily 9am–7pm. Free admission.*)

Moorish pottery at the Museu Islâmica in Mértola

of Succession, when the town was blown up in a series of massive explosions ordered by the Spanish Duke of Ossuña.

A wide staircase rises from the end of Praça da República (next to the very helpful tourist office) to a large plaza overlooking the town. A gate in the half-tumbled outer walls leads on into the courtyard of the castle, whose ramparts and towers you can explore for views over the whole town and a sense of how Serpa dominates the plains around it.

Serpa is 28km (17 miles) southeast of Beja. Tourist office: Praça da República. Tel: 284 544727.
Castle tel: 284 540100. Open: Mon 8am–1pm, Tue–Fri 8am–7pm, Sat 1–7pm. Closed: Sun. Free admission.

Mértola

Mértola stands at the highest navigable point on the Rio Guadiana, the river that divides Portugal from Spain for 100km (62 miles) or so, before it curves inland, leaving a rocky ridge of mountains to take over as the natural border. Phoenicians and Carthaginians sailed up as far as Mértola to trade, and the Romans established a permanent base there.

The remains of a Roman wharf can still be seen down by the waterside. For defensive reasons, the main part of the town is high above, on a hillside overlooking the river gorge and the confluence of the Oeiras tributary with the Guadiana.

The Moors left a much greater impact on the town. In the middle of Mértola is a domed mosque, one of only two known to have survived the zealous Christian assaults on infidel places of worship that took place after the expulsion of the Moors (the other is (Cont. on p94)

Tour: Prehistoric Alentejo

This circular motor tour of 75km (47 miles) takes in five prehistoric sites west of Évora, including a stone circle, the largest dolmen on the Iberian peninsula and cave paintings deep underground.

Allow 4 hours.

From Évora, take the N114 towards Montemor-o-Novo. After 10km (6 miles), leave the main road to turn left at the sign to Guadalupe.

1 Guadalupe

The small chapel on the right before the hamlet is the Capela de Guadalupe, founded in 1609. It was destroyed during a cyclone in 1941 but has since been restored.

Drive through Guadalupe to the junction at the far side: go straight across, following the sign to the Cromleque dos Almendres.

2 Cromleque dos Almendres

Follow the signs to drive through a fertile valley, past a Cooperativa Agrícola (Agricultural Cooperative). The road passes through an olive grove and ends abruptly at a picnic table. On the left is the cromlech – a circle of some 95 stones, arranged in an oval on a gentle slope and known locally as Pedras Talhas, 'Hewn Stones'.

Return through the olive grove to the Co-operative. Walk in front of the farmhouse towards the grain silos, following a blue arrow painted on the wall. Bear right at a broken wall heading towards an olive grove where the next menhir stands.

3 Menhir dos Almendres

The granite menhir stands 2.5m (8ft) tall – a remarkable intrusion into a peaceful landscape where your only companions are likely to be lapwings and cattle.

Return to the junction at Guadalupe and turn right to Valverde, passing the village wash-house and a sandy football pitch, driving along a ridged, compacted sand road. Cross a stream and drive through young eucalyptus trees. At the junction with a metalled road, opposite a café, turn left. Cross over the marshy river, passing a water tower, and turn left at the sign to Anta do Zambujeiro, passing through the yard of the agricultural station. Take the left-hand gate, recrossing the stream, and branch left again, following a sign for parking.

4 Anta do Zambujeiro

Leave your car here and cross the stream via the planks, heading towards the corrugated-iron shelter that has been built around this massive dolmen. The excavated finds from the site can be seen in the Museu de Évora.

Return through Valverde, continuing past the football pitch and a modern church with a large blue cross, into scarred countryside, which then gives way to vines and eucalyptus.

5 Anta do São Brissos

Beyond the turning to the village of São Brissos, another dolmen has been incorporated into the small chapel of São Brissos in the 17th century, accounting for the peculiar shape of its vestibule.

After another 5km (3 miles), the road joins the N370. Turn right, away from the village of Santiago do Escoural, for the underground paintings at the

Gruta do Escoural, just over 1km (²/₃ mile) away.

6 Gruta do Escoural

There is off-road parking in front of the high metal fence, whose gate will be locked if the custodian is not available to show you the paintings. The experience is not for the faint-hearted; from a small opening in the hillside a ladder descends into blackness which is only lit by the guide's light. You eventually reach a large chamber, inhabited by bats, and the guide traces the outline of horses on the walls.

On the return trip to Évora, via the N370 and N114, you can detour to visit the church at Nossa Senhora da Boa Fé.

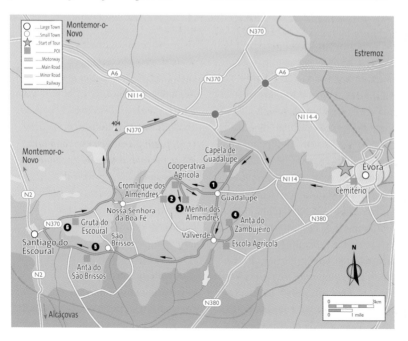

The headland overlooking Porto Covo

at Serpa). Follow signs to the 'Mesquita' which is now the parish church with statues of Christ and the Virgin looking out across 12 Moorish columns. The low, square crenellated building has been given a Renaissance doorway and a bell tower, but is nevertheless disorientatingly at odds with any other church in Portugal.

The castle walls are Moorish, too, built on Roman foundations. Within them, crowning the town, is a 13th-century keep. On display inside are pieces of carved stone from the Roman, Visigoth, Moorish and Christian eras, each of which left an influence on the castle. Roman and Islamic treasures are housed within several small museums including the **Museo Romano (Roman Museum)**, displaying excavations from a Roman house, the **Museu Islâmica (Islamic Museum)**, with a collection of pottery, glass and funerary stones, the **Museu de Arte Sacra (Museum of Religious Art)** and the **Basilica Paleocristã**, the remnants of an ancient Christian church preserving a collection of tombstones.

Birdwatchers are frequently to be found in Mértola, observing the storks; these have claimed the highest rooftops as nesting points, from where they glide over the gorge below. A flock of rare black vultures can also sometimes be

seen flapping over the town in search of the carrion that is left out for them.
Mértola is on the N122, 50km (31 miles) south of Beja.
Núcleos Museológicos de Mértola. Tel: 286 612443. Museums open: daily 9am–12.30pm & 2–5.30pm. Admission charge (combined ticket available).

Castro Verde

The pleasant provincial town has two main points of interest that make it worth leaving the main roads that intersect just outside it. **Basilica Real** (*open: Tue–Sun 10am–12.30pm & 2–6pm. Free admission*) sits at the town's highest point, its interior completely covered in *azulejos*. The upper layer of tiles is a series of panels showing scenes from the battle of Ourique, where Afonso Henriques's army defeated the far larger army of the Almoravid Moors, a victory that led to the beginnings of the Portuguese state.

More curious is the neo-Moorish folly on the main street, an astonishing pile with cantilevered galleries and exterior passageways overhanging the street, made to imitate intricate stone carving. Currently vacant, the future use of **Casa de Alvaro Romano Colaço** is uncertain.

Traffic roundabouts in Castro Verde are decorated with sculptures of life-sized farm animals that appear to be grazing on the grass. One of these is opposite the fairgrounds, where there is a working windmill.
Castro Verde is 46km (28½ miles) southwest of Beja. Tourist office: Praça
da Liberdade. Tel: 286 328148. Open: Mon–Fri 9am–12.30pm & 2–5.30pm, Sat & Sun 10am–1pm & 3–6pm.

Aljustrel

Bang in the middle of the Alentejo, Aljustrel has been an important centre of industry ever since the Romans discovered extensive reserves of copper in the area. The town itself is not particularly impressive, but there are three principal attractions here.

Castelo (Castle)

So little is left of Aljustrel's castle that the town's points of interest signs don't even mention it. Instead, follow signs to Senhora do Castelo, and climb the steps to find a few excavated foundations of the castle behind it. The site is a lovely and peaceful one, the stones interspersed with poppies. The climb up is rewarded with great views of the surrounding countryside and across the plains, over cork oak forest, cattle pasture and the blue water of a spindly shaped lake created by the Barragem do Roxo dam.

CORK

Forests of cork oak help break up the monotony of the landscape. Portugal is still the world's largest producer of cork. The difficult task of stripping the bark, without damaging the trunk, takes place in midsummer – but only after the tree has matured for about 40 years. The trees live for just over 150 years and are stripped at nine-yearly intervals, revealing the dark orange of their exposed trunks.

In the early evening, in particular, the Alentejo light can be crystal-clear, and the scattered villages stand out dazzlingly white in the wide open landscape.

Open: all day. Free admission.

Museu da Mina (Museum of Mining)

This interesting museum weaves together the geology and history of the area. It shows how Aljustrel lies at the end of a long belt of copper, stretching over to the great mines of Rio Tinto and Tharsis in Spain.

The Roman Empire's insatiable demand for bronze (an alloy of copper and tin) led it to exploit these reserves on a scale that has never been seen since. Roman mining tools are on display, along with explanations of how they extracted the metal from the ore. Remains from the large Roman necropolis nearby are also on show.

Tel: 284 601461. Open: all day. Free admission.

Nossa Senhora do Castelo

Beds of fragrant lavender and rosemary line the wide tiled stairs from the parish church to the hilltop chapel and former convent. In the early days, following the expulsion of the Moors, it stood as an important symbol of the victory of Christians over the infidel.

Tel: 284 600070. Open: all day. Free admission.

Aljustrel is 36km (22 miles) southwest of Beja on the N263. Tourist office:

Avenida 1 de Maio. Tel: 284 601010. Open: Jun–mid-Sept Tue–Sat 10am–12.30pm & 4–7pm, Sun 10am–1pm; mid-Sept–May daily 9.30am–12.30pm & 2–5.30pm.

Miróbriga

Miróbriga is one of Portugal's most outstanding archaeological sites. A settlement is thought to have been founded here by Celtic migrants in the 4th century BC. From the pottery and coins of this era found on the site, it is evident that it became an important centre of trade, with links across southern Spain. Even so, it is the remains of the 1st-century AD Roman city that provide the most palpable sense of the past. It is well worth wandering around the site for half an hour to get acclimatised before viewing the excavations in detail.

A large part of this great Roman city remains unexcavated and lies under the bumpy, pitted green hills of the site, but the 25,000-capacity amphitheatre, where citizens would have watched horse racing, gives a clue to its full dimensions. So, too, does the bathhouse, which is in a much better state of repair; plumbing experts can marvel at the water-heating system and the pipes that filled the cold, tepid and hot baths. At the highest point on the site are the relics of temples to Venus and Aesculapius. Many of the archaeological finds from Miróbriga are now in Santiago do Cacém's Museu Municipal.

Roman ruins at Miróbriga

Miróbriga is off the N120 road, signposted to Lisbon, about 1km (²/₃ mile) southeast of Santiago do Cacém. Open: Tue–Sat 9am–noon & 2–5.30pm, except public holidays. Admission charge.

Sines

The birthplace of Vasco da Gama, discoverer of the sea route to India, is a changed place these days. The character-filled old fishing town with its castle and sandy beach is now a deep-water port for oil tankers that feed the colossal (and colossally ugly) refinery. If you can get past this disfiguring ensemble, the old town still retains much of its charm and you can visit the **castle**, widely held to be the actual birthplace of Vasco da Gama. A colourful religious festival takes place during the first fortnight in August, reaching a climax on 15 August, the Feast of the Assumption.

Sines lies 20km (12 miles) southwest of Santiago do Cacém.
Sines Castle. Open: daily 9am–5pm. Admission charge.

Porto Covo da Bandeira

This is an enchanting little seaside village, on the Atlantic coast, that has retained its character in a way that

Fishermen's huts at Vila Nova de Milfontes

gaily painted wooden boats that put to sea from the port.

The coastline is broken splinter-like in both directions into cliffs, secluded coves and inlets, fine sandy beaches and rocky outcrops. Just visible to the south, about 1km (^{2}/$_3$ mile) out to sea, is an island known as Ilha do Pessegueiro ('Peach Tree Island').

There's usually a fisherman on the beach willing to take people across for a negotiated fee, but you will not find fruit trees of any description there – the island is entirely barren. However, there is a small ruined fortress and harbour to be explored as you play at being Robinson Crusoe. The fortress was built in the 17th century as a base for pre-emptive strikes against the pirates who lurked offshore, waiting to attack the coastal villages of the Alentejo. It was badly damaged in the same earthquake of 1755 that razed Lisbon to the

would be quite impossible if it were in the Algarve. The sea tends to be a few degrees cooler than on the south coast and a strong wind can blow from the north at any time of year. Despite this, Porto Covo satisfies the yearnings of people looking for a quiet and characterful fishing port.

The low, Moorish-influenced houses are uniformly whitewashed and have red-tiled roofs and sea-blue borders round their doors and windows. If you wend your way through the leafy main square and along spotlessly clean cobbled streets, you will come down to the seafront with its handful of shops and beach bars; here you can eat barbecued fish or octopus, fresh off the

THE HERMIT OF PORTO COVO

An oft-repeated legend in Porto Covo tells of a hermit who lived on the offshore island and was much revered for his holiness. Pirates attacked the island, killed the hermit and made a fire of his few possessions, which included a carved wooden image of the Virgin.

When fishermen subsequently sifted through the ashes, they found the Madonna unscathed. They took it to the mainland and built a chapel to Nossa Senhora da Queimada (Our Lady of the Burning), which later became a pilgrimage destination.

ground, and now survives only as a romantic ruin.

Porto Covo da Bandeira is 6km (4 miles) off the N120, which leads southwards from Sines to the Algarve.

Vila Nova de Milfontes

Vila Nova de Milfontes is the Alentejo's busiest seaside holiday resort. Although its scale pales in comparison to the mammoth developments of the Algarve, this quaint and attractive old fishing port is hugely popular with people from Lisbon and the Alentejo hinterland. Standing on the sandy north bank of the wide estuary of the Rio Mira, the resort has the advantage of long stretches of superb beach and a choice of either the Atlantic or the warmer, calmer estuary for swimming and watersports.

Although surrounded by a few modern hotels, the old town still oozes character. Narrow streets that wind down to the shore are lined by white-washed houses decorated in brightly coloured trim, and sprinkled with little restaurants serving the freshest of seafood. The 16th-century fort, which is now a hotel and not open to non-residents, has a fascinating history dating back to the times when Milfontes was in constant danger from piracy. Arab pirates would lurk off the coast waiting to plunder the town or kidnap its inhabitants, to be held for ransom or sold as slaves back in North Africa. King João's answer to the defence of Milfontes was to declare the town a safe haven for all Portuguese fugitives evading the law; in return, they had to agree to stay in the town and defend the castle whenever it came under attack.

Vila Nova de Milfontes is 41km (25 miles) south of Sines.
Tourist office: Rua António Mantas. Tel: 283 996599. Open: Mon–Fri 10am–12.30pm & 2–5pm, Sat 10am–12.30pm.

The sandy Rio Mira estuary

Upper Alentejo

The Alentejo's northern expanses, just south of the Tejo (Tagus) River, are not as heavily settled as Portugal's coastal regions. Here towns are separated by long stretches of open grassland where cattle graze and golden fields of grain ripen in the hot summer sun. Wild flowers paint the roadsides from March until summer weather sets in.

The motorway from Lisbon to Badajoz, just across the border in Spain, has brought more visitors to the northern section of the Alentejo. And the classification of the walled centre of Évora as a UNESCO World Heritage Site has brought it well-deserved attention. But the wide open spaces of the Alentejo still predominate, and many places are still waiting to be discovered. Once away from the motorway and Évora, lodging is not plentiful, but *pousadas* (government-run hotels) and some lovely country estates provide upmarket options, and larger towns usually have modest hotels or B&Bs.

Although many of the larger towns can be visited by road or rail, a car really is essential for discovering the Alentejo. Unless you like it roastingly hot, spring and autumn are the best times to visit.

It has been suggested that future years will see leisure parks in the Alentejo, with watersports on artificial lakes, irrigated golf courses and luxury hotel complexes. Until then, hilltop towns like Monsaraz and Estremoz can expect their views to change only with the seasons.

Farming is still the local economic base. The grain crops grown in this region earn it the title of 'The granary of Portugal', and Alentejo wines from Borba and elsewhere are gaining international attention. The land becomes more rugged north and east of Portalegre as it rises to the Serra de São Mamede. These steep mountains and valleys are part of a natural park, with hiking routes marked throughout. Some of Portugal's most appealing castellated towns, such as Marvão and Évora Monte, sit at the crests of these hills.

Évora

In 1986, UNESCO declared Évora a World Heritage Site, in recognition of the fabulous collection of architectural gems tightly clustered within this walled town. There are innumerable points of

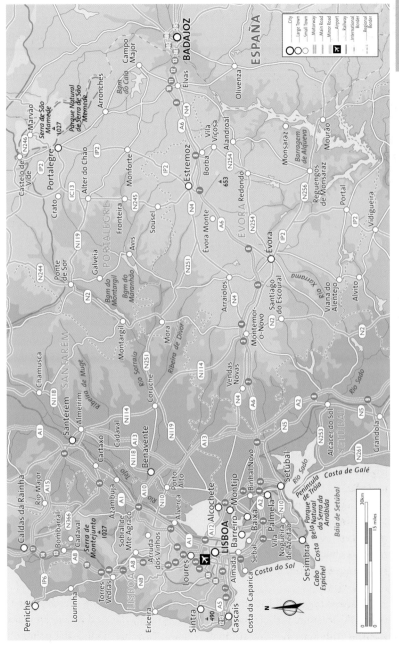

historical interest to detain sightseers as they wander along the stone-paved streets that link the city's many squares, where students from the university sit strumming guitars or leafing through textbooks. Many of the finest buildings are floodlit after dark, making for a romantic evening tour (*see pp106–7*).

Convento dos Lóios

The conventual quarters of this 15th-century monastery have been converted into a *pousada*. Guests now sleep in the old monastic cells, while two sides of the cloister have been turned into the dining area and the chapterhouse serves as a lounge. The **church of São João Evangelista** (St John the Evangelist) adjoins the monastery and is worth seeing for the beautiful *azulejo* tiles that line the nave. They were painted by António de Oliveira Bernardes, whom many experts consider to be the finest of all Portuguese tile artists.
Largo Marquês de Marialva. Tel: 266 704051. Church open: Tue–Sun 9am–12.30pm & 2–6pm. Admission charge.

Igreja de São Francisco

This 15th-century church features on the itinerary of most visitors because of its extraordinary **Capela dos Ossos (Chapel of Bones)** decorated with designs made from the bones of 5,000 human skeletons. Skulls grin at you from the walls and the ceiling, while the shrivelled corpses of a man and a child hang at the far end of the chapel. An inscription in Portuguese translates as: 'We bones lie here waiting for yours.' Although the macabre chapel revolts many people, it also seems to exercise an irresistible magnetism.

The chapel is approached through the chapterhouse in which wax images of arms, feet, breasts and other appropriate parts of the anatomy have been placed by way of offerings for people suffering injuries, disease or infertility.

At the chapel entrance, braids of human hair have been pinned to the wall; these are placed as votive offerings by young brides-to-be before their weddings.
Rua da República. Tel: 266 704521. Open: Mon–Sat 9am–1pm & 2.30–5.30pm, Sun 10am–12.45pm & 2.30–5.30pm. Admission charge.

Museu de Évora (Municipal Museum)

This museum, housed in the 17th-century former archbishop's palace, is one of the best in Portugal, renowned for its sculpture (from Roman to modern) and its medieval works of art. The star of the museum is the cathedral altarpiece, 13 panels dating to around 1500, depicting the Life of the Virgin.
Largo Conde de Vila Flor. Tel: 266 702604. Open: Tue 2.30–6pm, Wed–Sun 10am–6pm. Closed: Mon. Admission charge.

Paço dos Duques de Cadaval (Palace of the Dukes of Cadaval)

A short way downhill from the Roman temple is this 14th-century palace topped by a pair of imposing crenellated

Sturdy 16th-century towers rising above the façade of Évora's cathedral

towers, one of which formed part of the old city walls. Inside is a small art gallery exhibiting rows of stony-faced ancestral portraits along with some historic family documents. More interesting and beautiful are the splendid painted ceiling and the pair of 15th-century Flemish bronze commemorative plaques.
Largo Marquês de Marialva.
Open: Tue–Sun 9am–12.30pm &
2–6pm. Admission charge.

Sé (Cathedral)
The façade of the 12th- and 13th-century cathedral looks down on Largo Marquês de Marialva and the city's Roman temple, built 1,000 years previously. The two huge and sturdy fortress-like towers were added in the 16th century; they are strangely dissimilar since only one of them is topped with turrets.

The intricately sculpted stone statues of the Apostles, guarding the main entrance, are well worth a look. Inside there are three great naves and a soaring vaulted ceiling from which hang some enormous chandeliers. Don't miss the beautiful octagonal dome above the transept or the wooden stalls of the choir, carved in Renaissance style, reached by a staircase at the back.

The same staircase gives access to the cathedral's **Museum of Sacred Art,**

Évora (*see pp106–7 for walk route*)

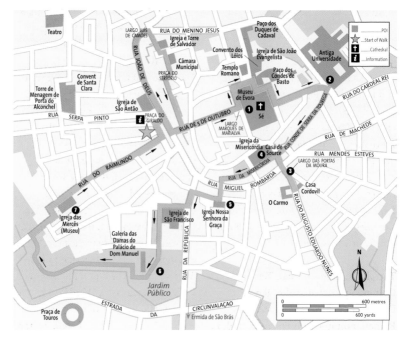

where the ageing custodian in faded uniform might show you photographs of himself in the company of Queen Elizabeth II, former US president Ronald Reagan and various other heads of state whose visits to Portugal included the mandatory tour of Évora. The museum houses an extensive collection of bejewelled gold and silver chalices and crucifixes, and some unbelievably ornate ecclesiastical vestments and mitres. The most extraordinary exhibit is an ivory carving of the Virgin of Paradise, believed to have been sculpted in the 13th century. The statue opens up to reveal three minutely carved scenes of the Annunciation, the Nativity and the Assumption of the Virgin into heaven.

Adjacent to the cathedral is the 14th-century Gothic cloister of carved granite. Worn and narrow stone staircases at each corner lead up to a terrace that looks down on the cloister and its small enclosed garden; there are also fine views over the town from the crenellated walls of the terrace.
Largo Marquês de Marialva.
Tel: 266 759330. Open: daily 9am–noon & 2–5pm; tower and cloister close 10min earlier. Museum. Open: Tue–Sat 9–11.30am & 2–4pm. Admission charge. Cumulative ticket available for cathedral, cloister and museum.

Templo Romano (Roman Temple)
Commonly known as the 'Temple of Diana', this is the most outstanding Roman monument in Portugal. Built in the 1st century AD, the Corinthian-style temple of marble plinths and granite columns stands in the middle of Largo Marquês de Marialva in the shadow of the grey Gothic cathedral. Over the centuries, the temple has been partly dismantled and used as a convenient source of building material for other city monuments. Six columns, however, remain perfectly intact; its usefulness as a medieval marketplace and, until 1870, as the city's municipal abattoir, probably prevented its total destruction.
Largo Marquês de Marialva.

Évora is on the N18, 46km (29 miles) southwest of Estremoz.
Tourist office: Praça do Giraldo.
Tel: 266 777071. Open: Nov–Mar daily 9am–6pm; Apr–Oct daily 9am–7pm.

Évora Monte
The castle and the tiny village of Évora Monte, sitting inside its encircling walls atop a steep hill, command one of the most spectacular panoramas in the Upper Alentejo. Expansive 360-degree views take in the two towns and boundless plains dotted with white villages. For this alone, an energetic scramble or an engine-straining 1.5km (1-mile) drive to the top is well rewarded.

Évora Monte is where the peace treaty was signed in 1834 ending the so-called 'War of the Two Brothers', the civil war fought between Pedro IV and his brother Miguel. This was one of the most
(*Cont. on p108*)

Walk: Évora

Capital of the Alentejo, Évora is one of the most elegant and historic cities in Portugal – a fact recognised by its UNESCO World Heritage Site status. This walking tour (see map on p104) covers the principal monuments.

Allow 2 hours.

Start at the Praça do Giraldo, at the geographical and commercial heart of the city, an elegant oblong bounded by balconied buildings and with a 16th-century fountain overlooked by the Renaissance São Antão church. Follow Rua de 5 de Outubro to the Largo Marquês de Marialva.

1 Largo Marquês de Marialva

Here is Évora's great assembly of historic buildings: to the right the cathedral; ahead the former episcopal palace, now the Museu de Évora; to the left the Roman Temple (Templo Romano) and the Convento dos Lóios, now one of the country's best-located *pousadas* (state-owned hotels). Further to the left, the Paço dos Duques de Cadaval (Palace of the Dukes of Cadaval) and its art gallery stand below the small formal park with its war memorial, collection of statues and good views from the terrace.
Walk under an arch behind the cathedral apse, passing a Gothic building known as the 'Mansion of the Counts of Portalegre'. Turn left and follow the street to the university.

2 Antiga Universidade

The 16th-century university has a two-tier cloister, and the classrooms leading off it are decorated with *azulejo* panels depicting the various subjects taught.
In front of the university, turn sharply right and follow Rua Conde de Serra da Tourega; halfway along, on the right, note the house dated 1866 and covered with tiles. At the next square, bear left into Largo das Portas da Moura.

3 Largo das Portas da Moura

At the far end of this square is the Casa Cordovil, with its elegant Manueline and Moorish balcony, roughly contemporary with the square's globe-shaped fountain (the symbol of King Manuel I's growing empire). In the opposite direction, two towers from the original city walls stand in front of the house of the Renaissance scholar Garcia de Resende.

Turn left at De Resende's house, continuing down Rua da Misericórdia, to the Misericórdia church.

4 Igreja da Misericórdia

This church is often closed: if it is open (before Mass is a good time to try), the sacristan will be happy to show you the ornate tiled interior, the gilded altar and, upstairs, the vestments and small museum.

Continue through the small square, taking the second stepped passage down into the square to the left.

5 Igreja Nossa Senhora da Graça

The façade of this small church has a flamboyant display of Renaissance sculpture topped with four giants.

Leave the square, taking Rua da República to Praça 1 de Maio, where the church of São Francisco houses the macabre Capela dos Ossos (see p102). Follow the road south to enter the Jardim Público (Public Gardens).

6 Jardim Público

To the right of the bandstand, paired Moorish windows line the so-called Galeria das Damas do Palácio de Dom Manuel. This is illuminated at night and stands near the remains of an earlier palace. The gardens follow part of the city's 17th-century fortifications; from the walls, you can see the turreted 15th-century Ermida (Hermitage) de São Brás, where the sentences of the Inquisition were meted out, and the bullring (Praça de Touros).

Leave the park by the gate in Rua do Raimundo and turn right to reach the Igreja das Mercês.

7 Igreja das Mercês (Museu)

This church, built in 1669, has been transformed into the museum of decorative arts, noted for its collection of *azulejos.*

Continue up Rua do Raimundo to Praça do Giraldo. To see some of the best arcaded streets, take Rua João de Deus to Largo Luís de Camões; return to Rua de 5 de Outubro via the Igreja e Torre de Salvador, the Câmara Municipal and the Praça do Sertório.

The spectacular cathedral tower at Évora

important events in recent Portuguese history and that may be why the authorities have seen fit to rebuild the once derelict **castle** keep, creating a four-storey reconstruction of the medieval original in painted cement. From a distance, it looks like a giant sandcastle with four large circular towers. Fortunately, this is not an experiment that has been repeated anywhere else in the Alentejo; it proves only that it is possible to ruin a good ruin.

Inside is a rather strange collection of exhibits, including reconstructed looms illustrating the traditional carpet-weaving industry of the region. More appropriately, there are displays of historical documentation explaining how the original castle was captured from the Moors in the 12th century and how an earthquake destroyed it in 1531, following which it was rebuilt with the thick-set towers reproduced so incongruously in the late 20th century. However, the crumbling ramparts, the old town gate, the church and the one-street village retain some of Évora Monte's ambience.

Évora Monte is signposted off the N18 halfway between Évora and Estremoz. Évora Monte Castle: Rua da Convencão. Tel: 268 395277. Open: summer daily 10am–1pm & 2.30–6.30pm; off-season daily 10am–1pm & 2.30–5pm. Admission charge.

Lago do Gadanha (Scythe Lake), Estremoz

Estremoz

A day or two spent in fortified, hilltop Estremoz is likely to prove one of the highlights of a visit to southern Portugal (for a walking tour of the town, *see pp110–11*). The town's castellated hilltop enclave has an ancient, otherworldly feel. No visitors experience this more intensely than those who stay in the grandiose 13th-century royal castle at the uppermost part of town; this has now been turned into the **Pousada da Rainha Santa Isabel** (*tel: 268 332075; reservations essential*). The rooms in this national monument are an extraordinary blend of the sumptuous and the spartan; there are enormous four-poster beds and bathrooms of marble quarried from the hills nearby, as well as expanses of bare stone wall with lanterns hanging from ceilings high above.

Even if you are not staying at the *pousada*, the reception staff will probably be happy to show you around; if not, you should at least climb the great marble staircase from the cavernous hall – the views from the dining room out over the plains of the Alentejo are stupendous.

Rising above the royal palace is the **castle keep**, with its white marble 'Tower of the Three Crowns' (a trio of kings all contributed to its construction). A steep, worn staircase leads up to a gallery from where you can see Évora, across the plains, and over to Spain in the east. Also in the castle is the enchanting **Rainha Santa Isabel Chapel**, bedecked with *azulejo* tiles depicting the life of this generous queen and saint who died in Estremoz in 1336, after devoting her life to the poor.

Estremoz is 44km (27 miles) northeast of Évora and 57km (35 miles) south of Portalegre. Tourist office: Rossio Marques de Pombal. Tel: 268 333541. www.estremozmarca.com. Keep and chapel open: daily 9–11.45am & 2–5.45pm, except Mon & public holidays. Admission charge.

Vila Viçosa

This royal city was once the seat of the Dukes of Bragança, the family that provided Portugal with its monarchs from 1640 until the proclamation of the republic in 1910. The city's regal buildings provide a very striking

contrast to the medieval fortified hilltops and Moorish-influenced architecture that characterise most of the Alentejo. Vila Viçosa (literally 'Shaded Town') is dominated by the magnificent three-storey Paço Ducal (Ducal Palace). This overlooks an expansive marble-paved square, with its statue of João IV, the first of the Bragança kings. Streets lined with orange trees lead to the outlying plains that were once covered with great tracts of prime hunting forest; this is usually offered as the reason why the Bragança dukes chose the town as their principal residence. Nowadays, Vila Viçosa is essentially a museum town, as evidenced by the rows of tour coaches parked in the square and the packs of escorted groups filing through the palace.

Paço Ducal (Ducal Palace)

The 110m (361ft) -long, white marble façade of the palace forms one side of the main square. Visitors waiting at the (*Cont. on p112*)

The royal city of Vila Viçosa

Walk: Estremoz

Arriving from the rolling plains at this, one of the Alentejo's most striking hilltop castle ensembles, brings a true sense of discovery. Estremoz is a historic market town where thorough exploration will give you a real insight into the history and present-day life of this region (see pp108–9).

Allow 2 hours.

Start from the Rossio, the main square. Cross to the smaller adjoining square to the north, dominated by a great expanse of water (or concrete, when the pond is empty).

1 Lago do Gadanha

The 17th-century Lago do Gadanha ('Scythe Lake') is named after the implement that Neptune waves above his head, in the middle of the pond. The church on the corner adjoining the Rossio is the Igreja de São Francisco (Church of St Francis) – originally part of a friary founded in the 13th century. Inside the Gothic church look for the tomb of Vasco Esteves Gato and a later Tree of Jesse.
Leave the church and turn right into Largo de Dom José I, heading for the Palácio Tocha at the northern junction with Rua 31 de Janeiro.

2 Palácio Tocha

Step inside the entrance hall of the 17th-century palace with its fine

vaulted ceiling and *azulejo* tiles depicting the War of Independence against Spanish rule. Rua 31 de Janeiro and Rua das Flores lead to the bullring (Praça de Touros) and the ancient town gate, the Portas de Santa Catarina.
Return to the lake and, passing the Fonte das Bicas, a fountain in the shape of a pine cone, continue up Rua 5 de Outubro to the Praça Luís de Camões.

3 Praça Luís de Camões

The fortifications of the upper town loom high above this square and its Manueline *pelourinho* (pillory).
Take the narrow pathway that branches left off Rua Vasco da Gama after a couple of minutes; the path climbs sharply to the left and rejoins the road as it enters the upper town through the Arco de Santarém, leading to the Largo do Castelo.

4 Largo do Castelo

The elegant Largo do Castelo (Castle Square) is bordered by historic buildings and dominated by the grey Torre de Menagem. Part of this castle and palace complex has been converted into the Pousada da Rainha Santa Isabel, one of the best in the country. Within the castle is a chapel dedicated to Rainha Santa Isabel (Queen St Isabel, wife of King Dinis, both of whom lived in the castle in the 14th century). The chapel is decorated with beautiful *azulejos* depicting the life of Isabel. Alongside the castle is the 16th-century Igreja (Church) de Santa Maria.

Follow the ancient narrow street, Rua do Cadria, which leads away from the Igreja de Santa Maria, ending at the Arco da Frandinha. A sign directs you from here, down Rua da Frandinha, back to the Praça Luís de Camões. Cross this square to reach the Rossio with the vast façade of the Câmara Municipal (Town Hall) ahead of you.

5 Câmara Municipal

This 17th-century building was originally built as a convent dedicated to St Philip Neri and contains fine *azulejo* depictions of scenes from his life. On the eastern side of the Rossio is another former convent, the cloister of the Misericórdia and Cruzeiro, now a hospital. Next door is the **Museu Rural**, whose displays provide a comprehensive insight into the traditional ways of Alentejan life (*Open: 10am–1pm & 3–6pm, except Mon and holidays. Admission charge*).

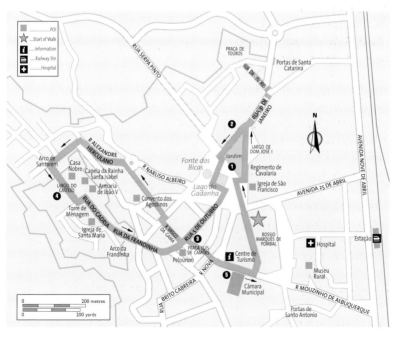

entrance for their guided tour will first see a series of huge paintings that depict some of Portugal's greatest military triumphs. The palace is now entirely a museum filled with fine art, porcelain, tapestries and other treasures of the royal era.

The halls of the main wing are hung with vast tapestries glorifying the 15th-century Age of Discovery, when Portugal was at the forefront of exploration in Asia and the Americas. There are also some superb 17th-century *azulejo* tiles on the walls, while the ceilings are painted with biblical and mythological scenes, such as the story of David and Goliath and the adventures of Perseus in the Underworld. From the great stone window frames, you can look out over the immaculately tended gardens, where peacocks strut amid the topiary.

In the adjacent transverse wing are the royal apartments, last used by King Carlos I, the penultimate Portuguese monarch, who left Vila Viçosa for Lisbon on 1 February 1908, along with his eldest son, the heir to the throne. They were both assassinated along the route. The younger son, Manuel II, reigned briefly before being forced into exile in England in 1910; there he died in 1932, leaving all his wealth, including the treasures of Vila Viçosa, to the Portuguese nation.

Two other points of interest in the palace are the collection of royal carriages and the kitchens; here, enormous gleaming copper cauldrons and huge roasting spits evoke the era of royal hunting and feasting.

Paço Ducal. Tel: 268 980659. Open: Oct–Mar Wed 10am–1pm & 2–5pm, Thur–Fri 9.30am–1pm & 2–5pm; Apr–Sept Tue 2–5pm, Wed–Fri 10am–1pm & 2.30–5.30pm, Sat & Sun 9.30am–1pm & 2.30–6pm. Last visits one hour before closing time.

The Amoreira Aqueduct, near Elvas

Old Elvas

Vila Viçosa is on the N255, 18km (11 miles) southeast of Estremoz. Tourist office: Praça da República. Tel: 268 881101.

Elvas

Just 10km (6 miles) from the Spanish border, Elvas has the feel of a frontier town. Spanish car number plates are ubiquitous. The nondescript new part of town is stuffed with restaurants where motorists travelling between Madrid and Lisbon stop for their first (or last) meal for which they pay Portuguese rather than (the much higher) Spanish prices.

Old Elvas, across the road, could not form a more striking contrast. Within the redoubtable ramparts, broken only by sturdy stone gateways, are stone-paved streets, low arches and quaintly tumbledown whitewashed houses with iron-grilled windows and pots of

flowers standing outside. Over centuries of hostility with Spain, strategic Elvas became known as a *chave do reyno* – 'key to the kingdom' – and its formidable fortifications were no mere gesture of defiance: in 1644, during the War of Restoration, and again in 1659, Elvas withstood massive Spanish assaults. In 1801, it was despite the successful resistance of Elvas that the Portuguese capitulated to Spain after the Spanish had declared war over Portugal's refusal to break her alliance with the British. Ten years later, Wellington launched his siege of Badajoz from Elvas.

The joy of the old town is that it is still very much a lived-in quarter, with washing hanging out to dry, children playing football in ancient courtyards, and drivers hooting furiously as they get stuck in impossibly narrow entrances. Sights not to miss are the

Portalegre and its cathedral

16th- and 17th-century Aqueduto da Amoreira (Amoreira Aqueduct), which brought water to the town from 7.5km (4¹/₂ miles) away, the marble pillory in the triangular Largo Santa Clara, the mosaic paving in the Praça da República main square, and the views over to Spain from the top of the ramparts, next to the castle.

Elvas is on the N4 road to Madrid, 10km (6 miles) from the Spanish border. Tourist office: Praça da República, by the bus stop. Tel: 268 622236. www.cm-elvas.pt. Open: Mon–Fri 9am–12.30pm & 2–5.30pm, Sat & Sun 10am–12.30pm & 2–5.30pm.

Portalegre

The capital of the Upper Alentejo, located near the northern extremity of the province, is a small but bustling town in the foothills of the Serra de São Mamede mountain range, surrounded by green countryside that contrasts sharply with the sun-burnt plains further south. King Dinis fortified the town in 1290 because of its proximity to the Spanish border. In 1704, it fell briefly to the Spanish during the Spanish War of Succession; then, during the Peninsular War, it was held by Napoleon's troops. Remains of the castle survive, and an impressive section of the medieval city walls encloses the oldest of the city's vertiginous streets. Portalegre's prosperity in the 15th–17th centuries was based on silk and wool weaving, an industry that accounts for the many fine mansions that line its streets.

Museu Municipal

This small museum, housed in the 18th-century former diocesan seminary just behind the cathedral, contains several collections: snuffboxes, Chinese porcelain and ivory carvings, gold and silver chalices and crucifixes,

and a beautiful 17th-century tabernacle carved in ivory.
Praça do Município, Câmara Municipal. Tel: 245 302544. Open: Wed–Mon 9.30am–12.30pm & 2–6pm. Closed: Tue. Admission charge.

Museu da Tapeçaria (Tapestry Museum)

The art of fine tapestry, established here in 1947 and for which Portalegre is now known in international art circles, is chronicled in the excellent tapestry museum. The workshop is housed in a 17th-century former Jesuit seminary, where visitors can follow the extraordinary process on a 45-minute guided tour.

No two tapestries are alike. Many of them are copies of paintings, or even photographs, reproduced from a palette of nearly 8,000 different shades of wool and painstakingly stitched to create a wonderfully tactile version of the original.
Rua da Figueira. Tel: 245 307530. Open: Tue–Sun 9.30am–1pm & 2.30–6pm. Closed: Mon. Admission charge.

Sé (Cathedral)

The huge cathedral is never out of sight, its pinnacles towering above the city. It was begun in the 16th century in Renaissance style, while the façade, of wrought-iron balconies and marble pillars, was added in the 18th century. The cavernous, triple-naved interior can be refreshingly cool on a summer's day; ask to see the 18th-century

azulejo tiles in the sacristy, illustrating the Flight into Egypt. Fine paintings and altarpieces are in several of the side chapels.
Praça do Município. Open: daily. Free admission.

Portalegre is on the N359, 57km (35 miles) north of Estremoz and 81km (50 miles) northwest of Elvas. Tourist office: Rua Guilherme Gomes Fernandes 28. Tel: 245 307445.

Castelo de Vide

Rising from a spacious main square, Castelo de Vide's steep old quarter is a maze of narrow streets that once made up the Judiaria, the medieval Jewish district. Look for the low doorways with graceful double-curved ogival arches and other stonework, and see the synagogue, one of the few from that period remaining in Portugal.

These streets climb steeply to the castle (*open: May–Oct daily 9am–7pm; Nov–April daily 9am–5pm*), rebuilt in 1310, inside whose walls is a charming little neighbourhood of whitewashed homes. Climb the keep for views of the town, the mountains and into Spain. To sample Castelo de Vide's spring water, long famed for its restorative powers, look for the Fonte da Vila, covered by a roof supported on graceful stone columns.
Tourist office: Praça Dom Pedro V. Tel: 245 901361. Open: daily Jun–Aug 9am–7pm; Sept–May 9am–12.30pm & 2–5.30pm.

Marvão

'You have Portugal at your feet and, in opening your arms, Spain', wrote the Portuguese poet José Amaro of Marvão. It is apparent, from a long way away, why Marvão became one of the most strategic fortified positions on Portugal's eastern flank. Situated on one of the highest peaks of the São Mamede ridge that forms a natural border with Spain, this medieval town has dominating views over Spain to the east and as far as Portugal's highest mountain range, the Serra da Estrela, to the north. All around are cliffs sheer enough to make the town virtually unassailable.

A narrow road leads up to the craggy summit, where Marvão perches. Within the walls there is only a handful of tightly clustered houses, mainly because the town never had any real function, other than as a garrison. A walk round the walls is a delightful way to spend half an hour, as is a stroll through the steep, winding streets.

Over the centuries, the former Moorish stronghold was on the front line of Portugal's struggle to win and maintain independence from Spain. From 1640 to 1660, after the enemy from the east had been driven out and João IV sat on the throne, Marvão was relentlessly attacked by Spain in a vain attempt to reconquer Portugal. Napoleon's forces took the town at the start of the Peninsular War but were driven out in 1808.

Opposite the castle gate is one of the best local museums in the Alentejo, with a chapel lined in *azulejos*, examples of delicate handmade lace and extensive exhibits on the many nearby Bronze Age sites and their excavations. Ask at the adjacent tourist office for walking route maps of the neighbouring Serra da São Mamede. Below the town, near the river, the large Roman settlement of Ammaia emerges in an ongoing archaeological dig. A good little museum shows artefacts unearthed there.

Marvão is signposted off the N246, 24km (15 miles) north of Portalegre.
Tourist office: Largo de Santa Maria. Tel: 245 909131. www.cm-marvao.pt. Open: Mon–Fri 9.30am–5.30pm, Sat & Sun 9.30am–12.30pm & 2–5.30pm.

Monsaraz – the Igreja Matriz

View from the ramparts in the fortified village of Monsaraz

Monsaraz

Like many in the chain of fortified hilltops that runs along Portugal's eastern border with Spain, Monsaraz huddles entirely within its impregnable walls. So compact is this village, high above the Guadiana River and overlooking Spain, that even the main street is too narrow for a car. This adds to the distinctly medieval ambience that still pervades the place.

Because of its strategic position, Monsaraz was the site of a prehistoric settlement, then a Roman, Visigothic and Moorish village before being taken from the Moors in 1167. It was heavily fortified in the 14th century by King Dinis, when the formidable ramparts, square towers and castle were built. In front of the two-storey pentagonal keep is a square where bullfights are held on feast days, while villagers sit cheering from the surrounding stone walls.

The view from the parapets is stunning; the plains of the Alentejo stretch out endlessly towards the coast, whose outline just becomes visible on the horizon when it is exceptionally clear. The rocky, meandering Guadiana River, to the east, provides a dramatic contrast, while Spain extends beyond like a crumpled rug.

There are several points of interest on Rua Direita, the cobbled main street, which is lined with houses emblazoned with the coats of arms of wealthy 16th- and 17th-century families. Do not miss the Paços do Concelho Tribunal Building; this has a 15th-century fresco illustrating a judge being

Alvito – a classic little Alentejan town of sleepy streets and quiet squares

tempted by an impish, bribe-offering devil while simultaneously being drawn to the outstretched arms and majestic justice of Christ. An elaborately carved marble tomb in the Igreja Matriz (Parish Church) is worth a look.

Since the mid-1980s, full-bodied red wines from Reguengos de Monsaraz, 15km (9 miles) east, have achieved widespread acclaim, and are available in specialist wine shops around Europe. You can visit the **Cooperativa Agrícola de Reguengos de Monsaraz** to taste the wines or stock up.

Cooperativa Agrícola de Reguengos de Monsaraz. 5 Rua Conde de Monsaraz. Tel: 266 509310. Open: by prior appointment. Free admission.
Monsaraz is on the N319, 7km (4 miles) off the N256, between Évora and Mourão.

Mourão

This remote little town, on the east side of the Guadiana River, just 7km

(4 miles) from the Spanish border, is another in the string of fortified strongholds running down the country's eastern flank. Its name relates directly to a Moorish past but, curiously, the original town was located below the present site, down towards the river. Some say that river-borne disease drove the population uphill; others that it was the castle's indefensible position.

The neglected ruins of what is known as the Vila Velha (Old Town) are worth visiting for a ramble round the ramparts and the three towers, all that is left of the ancient castle.

Mourão is on the N256, 7km (4 miles) west of the frontier post at São Leonardo and 20km (12 miles) east of Reguengos de Monsaraz.

Alvito

As you approach Alvito across the expansive outlying plains, it appears as a classic little red-tiled and whitewashed

Alentejan town. Yet the characteristically sleepy town has a dazzling history, which is reflected in the rich atmosphere; this can be experienced by wandering the streets full of houses decorated with curvaceous arabesque ornament and by gazing up at the sturdy medieval castle.

The builders of the **Castelo de Alvito** were the Barons of Alvito who, for centuries, were among the most powerful of Portugal's aristocracy. Their castle was completed in 1482, shortly after the king had made this the first Barony in the country; he also allowed the first Baron of Alvito the unprecedented honour of owning his own castle – until then every castle in Portugal was the property of the king.

Unlike other fortresses of this era, Alvito Castle has, as well as defensive towers and crenellated parapets, a splendid Great Hall and several rooms with stone-carved arched windows. The Barony declined over the centuries and Alvito Castle fell into dereliction. Following imaginative and painstaking restoration, it reopened as an atmospheric 20-bedroom *pousada* in 1993.

For those who love to visit the local churches, don't miss the **Igreja Matriz de Nossa Senhora da Assunção**, located on Largo da Trindade. It is a lovely 16th-century Renaissance building (*open at the whim of the keyholder and for Sunday services*).

Alvito is 10km (6 miles) south of Viana do Alentejo and 28km (17 miles) *north of Ferreira do Alentejo on the N257.*

Viana do Alentejo

Bypassed by most tourists, because it is not served by any main roads, this little town has a small atmospheric castle and one of the most unusual and interesting churches in the Alentejo.

The **castle** could be straight out of a picture book. You can walk round the rectangular ramparts and battlements, linking four cylindrical towers, for views of the town and the plains beyond. Within the walls are some well-tended gardens with lawns and privet hedges.

The **church of Nossa Senhora da Assunção** is also fortified with crenellations, and with turrets in place of bell towers, so that from a distance church and castle appear to merge together into a single entity. Beneath the battlements of the façade, however, is a fine Manueline doorway.

The interior is an unusual mixture of Romanesque with Manueline

(*Cont. on p122*)

The battlemented church of Viana do Alentejo

Upper Alentejo

Family life

In Portugal, among both rich and poor, the family unit is exceptionally important and everyone feels a strong sense of kinship and loyalty towards it. In this Roman Catholic country, families are often large and embrace several generations. It is common for young children to be cared for by grandparents or by their older brothers and sisters. This is particularly true of rural areas because it enables both parents to work on the land.

All generations come together in a festival in Alte

Music and dancing at a family celebration in the Alentejo

The poverty of rural life means that children tend to live at home until they are married; even then, it is not uncommon for a newly married couple to move in with one set of parents.

In a peasant economy, shortage of land forces many parents to work especially hard in order to save and give a head start to their children. Working abroad, sometimes for several years, is one way of making vital extra money, and most families possess at least one member who is *lá fora* ('out there').

In the houses of the Algarve and the Alentejo, the kitchen is very much the centre of family life. The domestic economy is organised around the seasons and in such a way that nothing is wasted. If a pig is killed everybody participates and a use is found for every part of the animal.

Outside of the kitchen, there is not much division of labour by gender; socially, however, the local bar tends to be a male preserve while women will often be seen crocheting in groups outside their houses or in the town square. Women live longer than men, which explains the plenitude of old ladies dressed in black, the conventions of mourning still being widely observed.

embellishments. The roof is supported by octagonal, carved stone pillars. All the way round the base of the nave is a fringe of superb 17th-century *azulejo* tiles. Don't miss the rather splendid Crucifix in the chancel.

Viana do Alentejo is 29km (18 miles) south of Évora.

Alcácer do Sal

From Moorish times to the present day, the purest salt in Portugal has been extracted from the marshy land on either side of the flood-prone Sado River. The drawbridge, which once allowed small ships up to the saltworks, is nowadays permanently down. Rice, wheat and vegetables are also grown on the flat, fertile land that surrounds this historic and attractive little whitewashed riverside town, making it an important agricultural hub. Many motorists stop by the bridge to watch the numerous storks, which feed in the rice paddies and circle over the town before returning to their nests; these look like huge baskets perched on the tops of churches and towers. Rising on a hill above the medieval kernel at the town's heart is the 12th-century castle, built on the foundations of an earlier Moorish fortress and now converted into the lovely Pousada Dom Afonso II.

Within the walls is the small, dark and atmospheric Santa Maria (a 12th-century church that can provide a cool escape from the summer heat) and the 16th-century Aracelli convent now part of the *pousada*. The 16th-century Santiago Church, below the castle, is beautifully tiled in antique *azulejos*. Another church of this era, the Espírito Santo, houses a small archaeological museum exhibiting scraps of Roman, Phoenician and Moorish pottery among a collection of artefacts found in the area.

Alcácer do Sal is in the northwest corner of the Alentejo, 52km (32 miles) southeast of Setúbal.

Tróia Peninsula

The Tróia Peninsula is a long narrow spit jutting 20km (12 miles) out of the northwest corner of the Alentejo, towards the great industrial metropolis of Setúbal. To one side of this sandy, marshy promontory is the lake-like estuary of the Sado River, which the peninsula almost encloses; on the other side is the Atlantic.

The peninsula is lined with hotels and is a popular holiday resort, as well as a day-trip destination for the people of Lisbon and Setúbal. Beaches on the Sado estuary side of the promontory tend to be more crowded because the water is calmer and usually a couple of degrees warmer. However, dedicated sea bathers should make for the western side, only a few hundred metres away, where great Atlantic rollers frequently crash on to the sand.

The furthermost tip of Tróia is dominated by a huge, high-rise complex with hotels, restaurants, a golf course and every kind of watersports facility.

The beach is excellent, but it does get very crowded in the high season.

Cetóbriga

This is an interesting semi-excavated Roman site on the Sado estuary side of the peninsula. It was founded in the 1st century AD and grew into one of the most important fishing and fish-processing towns in the Roman Empire. Archaeologists believe that a tsunami, caused by an earthquake, was responsible for its destruction in the 5th century AD. However, the fish-processing tradition of the area has endured to the present day; in Setúbal, just across the water, this is a massive industry.

Ancient docks and fish-processing equipment have been unearthed at Cetóbriga and these can be viewed, along with a bathhouse, gymnasium, chapel and fragments of frescoes.

Cetóbriga is on the left bank of the Rio Sado, facing Setúbal. Open: Fri–Tue 9am–1pm & 3–6pm. Free admission.

Reserva Natural do Estuario do Sado (Sado Estuary Nature Reserve)

The reserve includes most of the land bordering on the estuary, as well as the base of the Tróia Peninsula. The habitat consists of marshland and mudflats, bordered by rolling banks of sand dune. The reserve is home to cranes, storks, egrets, all kinds of wildfowl and countless species of migratory birds. Dolphins and otters are also occasionally spotted in the estuary.

It is easily accessible by roads leading off the E52 north from Alcácer do Sal, and is best explored on foot; if armed with a pair of binoculars, so much the better.

The Tróia Peninsula is on the N253 west of Alcácer do Sal.

Interior of the Igreja do Santiago in Alcácer do Sal

Getting away from it all

The whole of the Alentejo region, with its sparsely populated hilltop villages and endless horizons, will appeal to the traveller in search of an escape from the crowds. The same cannot be said of the Algarve, but there is still far more to this region than a long beach backed by a furious highway. Of course, one way to get away from it all is to visit southern Portugal out of season – especially in the spring, when you will be able to enjoy the superb wild flowers as well as the absence of other visitors.

Other than that, there are plenty of opportunities to find peace, adventure or solitude on those days that you don't want to spend on a busy beach.

Adventure excursions

One way to explore the backroads and mountains of the Algarve is by joining an organised excursion, usually billed as a 'safari', travelling in a 4WD vehicle to explore the roughest terrain of the *serra* – the mountainous region separating the Algarve from the Alentejo. Several companies advertise in the main coastal resorts and out of Évora – ask for information at local tourist offices – and many offer big-game fishing trips, yacht charter or balloon flights as well. If you are interested, check their itineraries, and – most important – the insurance cover they offer. Some car rental companies offer 4WD jeeps if you want to make the trip independently. To see how the professionals do it, watching an off-road rally offers the excitement of racing in remote countryside: the largest

is the annual Transalgarve in March. If the roar of a straining jeep engine is not your idea of an escape, consider a journey on horseback instead. Look for signs to 'Centro Hípico'.

Beaches

Despite the popularity of the big names such as Albufeira, Praia da Rocha or Quarteira, substantial parts of the Algarve coast remain undeveloped. Some believe it may only be a matter of time before this situation changes, despite the introduction of new planning restrictions by the Portuguese government. Even so, west from Lagos, round Cabo de São Vicente (Cape St Vincent), and north as far as Sines, and again east of Faro, you can still find almost empty beaches, while only a few kilometres inland from these beaches you will discover peaceful, often unspoilt, landscapes.

The least developed beaches are those that stretch north from Cabo de São Vicente. Far from the larger towns and holiday resorts, and sometimes fairly inaccessible, this coast faces the full force of the Atlantic, making it colder and breezier than those around the headland to the south. Beaches such as Praia do Castelejo, Bordeira and Monte Clérigo offer magnificent stretches of windswept sand, backed by deep, wind-formed dunes. The surf is impressive, but be careful of strong currents. There are few facilities here, but most of the beaches have one or two cafés and the nearby villages have accommodation.

On the Alentejo coast, Vila Nova de Milfontes is popular with Lisboetas as well as tourists, but halfway between Milfontes and Sines – not the most attractive resort – the little village of

Porto Covo has its own Praia de Conches and lies near the small Ilha do Pessegueiro, which you can visit with a local boatman.

Islands

Many of the most remote beaches along the southern coast lie on offshore islands or along the sandbars that stretch for up to 12km (7 miles) in length all along the balmy *sotavento* (leeward) coast east of Faro. Some, especially those served by regular ferries, can get very busy in high season, while with others the only way to get there is to persuade a local fisherman to take you across (and pick you up again) by boat. Ilha de Tavira is a long sandy bar that can get crowded;

Alentejo coast at Zambujeira do Mar

Getting away from it all

quieter is Barril, which you can reach from Pedras del Rei. Both have long sandy beaches with warm water and can be reached by ferry. The Ilha de Faro can be reached by car along the causeway beyond the airport (signposted 'Praia de Faro'), or by ferry from the harbour, but it gets very busy in high season.

The islands off the port of Olhão can be reached by regular ferry in summer; the Ilha da Armona is the nearer, while the Ilha da Culatra, on which stands Faro's lighthouse, or *farol*, is quieter.

Boat trips

Instead of driving inland from the crowded beaches of the Algarve, try heading in the opposite direction – out to sea. There is a wide variety of trips on offer all along the southern coast, from a gentle ride up the Guadiana River from Vila Real de Santo António to a deep-sea shark-fishing trip, strictly for those with a strong constitution.

Fishing boats leave from many of the larger fishing ports, including Portimão and Vilamoura. Don't forget that the sun can be even fiercer out at sea than on the beach, while the wind can be more biting; sunblock and a sweater are a good combination.

A boat trip is also the best way to see the fascinating caves and grottoes formed along the *barlavento* (windward) section of the Algarve coast between Albufeira and Lagos. Trips depart from Benagil for the Carvoeiro section, from

Lagos or Praia Dona Ana for Ponta da Piedade, from Albufeira west to the Gruta do Xorino (which can also be reached on foot) and from Armação de Pêra for the Gruta do Pontal.

Mountain villages and lakes

It is not just the Alentejo that has remote mountain villages – though few in the Algarve have such dramatic approaches as those to Évora Monte and Monsaraz. Few tourists take time to explore the villages of the mountainous *serra* region, except perhaps for the popular and spectacular drive through the Serra de Monchique to Caldas and Fóia. The villages of the central and eastern Algarve, in particular, are little known and can present challenging driving, but it can be rewarding to visit a remote chapel or small market that few others reach.

In the northeast, the N124 leads into the mountains through one of the region's most rural – and beautiful – areas, with ancient villages, high mountain pastures, cool forests and long views. The N507 follows the banks of the meandering Guadiana River from Alcoutim through tiny hamlets such as Alamo and Foz de Odeleite.

Touring with a purpose, perhaps in search of *azulejos* or a particular market or festival, can take you deep into the back country of the *serra*; to remote villages such as Cachopo, an ancient place of pilgrimage that centres on its church of Santo Estêvão: festivals take place on the second Sunday in August

The Alvor estuary near Portimão – now declared a nature reserve

and 26 December, and the pilgrimage of Santo Estevão takes place on 20 and 21 September. From Cachopo, the N124 continues southwest to Barranco do Velho, by way of Vales and Feiteira, a route that offers some great views.

Inland lakes and reservoirs, usually named after their dam (*barragem*), are also popular destinations for bird-watchers, windsurfers and picnickers. The largest in the Algarve is the Barragem da Bravura, 15km (9 miles) north of Lagos in the foothills of the Serra de Espinhaço de Cão; for views of the water, head west from Monchique on the N267 to Aljezur, past unspoilt countryside to the coast, via the village of Marmelete. Further east, on the N124 from Silves to São Bartolomeu de Messines, is the turning for the Barragem de Arade.

There are many more reservoirs in the Alentejo, though the water level drops in summer, so don't expect them always to be as extensive as they appear on a map. One of the most attractive is the small Barragem de Tapada Grande on the N265, which crosses the Serra de Mértola and Serra de Serpa. Another is the Barragem de Santa Clara (also called the Barragem de Marcello Caetano), reached from the Algarve by heading north from Monchique on the N266.

Parks and gardens
Évora has its Jardim Público, complete with bandstand and elegant palace

Roman fish mosaic, Milreu

ruins, and the Ducal Palace at Vila Viçosa has its elegant topiary, but, on the whole, green parks and ornamental gardens are rare in southern Portugal. Another one worth searching out, in the Alentejo, is the garden of the old spa at Moura, built below the castle and with a wide variety of fountains, as well as a grand duck pond.

In the Algarve, one of the best places to seek solitude is among the palms and fountains at Estói, whose small park has some interesting ancient shrubs as well as some of the best ornamental stone-work in the country.

If you have children to amuse, try the gardens and the small zoo next to the castle at Silves. They may also enjoy a visit to the lush gardens of the São Lourenço Cultural Centre, outside Almancil, while you try to explain what the marble sculptures represent.

Some of the region's most luxuriant natural vegetation can be explored on a walk from the spa town of Caldas de Monchique.

Prehistoric and Roman remains

If getting away from modern life altogether sounds appealing, the landscapes of the Alentejo and the Algarve can reveal much of southern Portugal's long history. In the Alentejo, you can find some remarkable examples of prehistoric life deep in the countryside: try the tour on *pp92–3* to discover the ancient stone circle at Almendres, the menhir of Zambujeiro and the underground cave paintings at Escoural, or look for more Neolithic stones and dolmens around Monsaraz.

Even in the Algarve, among the modern holiday villas, you can find evidence of Roman and even earlier life in the southwest corner of Iberia. The megalithic grave at Alcalar can be viewed at ground level or from a walkway above. The remains of the Roman villa at Abicada, near Portimão, are overgrown and atmospheric in their abandonment. You can find lots more to follow up in the fascinating regional museums in Lagos and Faro, which display numerous artefacts from Neolithic, Bronze Age and Roman sites throughout the Algarve.

Further east, the Roman remains at Milreu and at Vilamoura are better preserved and easier to interpret, while the ruins of Balsa can be found near the Torre de Ares, a medieval watchtower 5km (3 miles) west of Tavira.

In the Alentejo, the Roman settlement of Miróbriga, near Santiago do Cacém, has been excavated and is one of Portugal's major Roman sites. The two-storey Roman farm villa at São Cucufate, north of Beja, and the extensive mosaics in the 40-room Roman villa at Pisões, also near Beja, show how prosperous Romans lived in the 1st to the 4th centuries.

Wildlife

Tourists were not the first temporary residents in southern Portugal: the Algarve in particular has long provided a rich variety of natural habitats which attract migrating birds. Despite the restrictions on hotel and resort

Temple of Diana, Évora

The Algarve is a birdwatcher's paradise

This is an important stopover and wintering point for migratory birds, as well as being rich in shellfish and a spawning ground for other fish. On a clear day, you get a particularly good view of the reserve as you come in to land at Faro airport. Contact the park headquarters (*Quinta de Marim, 3km (2 miles) east of Olhão. Tel: 289 704134*).

The sandy offshore islands east of Faro are particularly rich in birdlife, so ornithologists, as well as beach-seekers, should take the ferry across, especially in spring.

In the very southeastern corner of the Algarve, the Reserva Natural do Sapal de Castro Marim e Vila Real de Santo António lies between the Via Infante highway, the Guadiana River and the sea. It consists of salt marsh (*sapal*), which can be explored along a series of boardwalks. Like the Ria Formosa, it supports a wide range of birdlife; for information, go to the office located in the 13th-century fortress in Castro Marim, up Rua do Castelo from the central Praça 1 de Maio.

Moving west, another excellent area for birdwatching, and an important collection of habitats, lies between Portimão and Lagos, at the heart of the developed coastline. The successful campaign to raise the Alvor estuary to the status of a natural reserve has been a long one and there are still threats from development: the local economy depends on fishing, and lunching on fresh fish near the *lota*, or fish market,

development imposed by the Portuguese government, conservationists are concerned that many of those habitats are still under threat. A growing awareness in Portugal itself, where environmental groups (such as the LPN, Liga para a Protecção da Natureza) are becoming increasingly active, has led to the designation and protection of several areas, some of which welcome visitors.

Largest and best known is the **Parque Natural da Ria Formosa**, an area covering 17,000ha (42,000 acres), mostly of salt pans and lagoons stretching from Ançao to Cacela Velha.

at Alvor is popular with visitors; this is also a prime area for more hotel and golf course development.

The best way to explore the Ria de Alvor is to visit the A Rocha field studies centre at Cruzinha, which lies a short way south of the N125, opposite the turning to Mexilhoeira Grande. The centre publishes a range of ornithological literature, such as *An Atlas of the Wintering Birds in the Western Algarve.*

A smaller area of natural interest, which is very popular with Lagoans and visitors alike, is the Sítio das Fontes, an inlet from the Arade estuary which lies about 2km (1¹/₄ miles) from the turning to Estômbar village, between Lagoa and Portimão. Much more spectacular, Cabo de São Vicente (Cape St Vincent) has an abundance of both flora – particularly in spring – and birdlife; seabirds and migrating land birds use it as a landmark and staging post.

Further north, the underdeveloped coast of the western Algarve and the Alentejo are also ideal places for watching the wildlife undisturbed. Visitors should be warned, however: if they decide to explore more remote areas, whether in the Algarve or the Alentejo, this is a very popular hunting area, and even though the sport is theoretically restricted to Thursdays and Sundays when the season is on, stray gunshot is an all-too-real threat.

Getting away from it all

Cabo de São Vicente – renowned for its flora and birdlife

Shopping

The main challenge for the shopper in southern Portugal, particularly in the main tourist areas, is sorting out the quality goods from the tat. If you keep your eyes open, you can pick up some real bargains and some interesting local hand-crafted items, especially at local markets. Do not ignore roadside vendors: their handmade arts may be cheaper and better than the equivalent in shops. New to the retail scene are the mega shopping malls, especially at Faro, Guia and Portimão, providing international shops and cinemas.

WHAT TO BUY
Antiques

Antique objects, whether found in shops or in markets, tend to be expensive. Religious artefacts, old *azulejos* and Rato pottery predominate. **Casa da Papagaio** (*Rua de 25 Abril, Lagos*) is a store worth visiting for its vast and eccentric array of odds and ends. It is presided over by two green parrots and has a less spectacular sister shop in Portimão (*Rua Santa Isabel*).

Baskets

Baskets are something of an Algarvian speciality, but be sure to check that you are getting the real thing, since cheap Chinese imports now outnumber home-made products. Algarvian baskets are made from *esparto* grass, rushes or palm, and come in many shapes and sizes. The main centres for their manufacture are Aljezur, Monchique and the village of Odeleite.

Cork and ceramics

Cork is one of the south's main exports, but its transformation into an assortment of tourist souvenirs is one of its most tacky and least satisfactory manifestations. Happily, a recent addition to the cork repertoire has been its use as a material for smart and tasteful handbags, wallets, notebooks and backpacks. Ceramics are a safer bet, with a fair variety of styles ranging from ubiquitous pottery roosters to antique *azulejos*. The local wares include simple terracotta kitchen vessels from the Algarve, decorative pieces from the Alentejo illustrated with naively painted scenes from everyday life, and, from Estremoz, small figurines of saints and famous Portuguese characters.

These are sold everywhere, but there is a concentration of potteries along the N125 near Porches. The best examples of the delicate local floral-patterned wares can be found at Porches Pottery and Olaria Pequena.

Food and wine

The many sweetmeats and pastries of the south make excellent presents, especially when nicely wrapped, as do the local almonds and various dried fruits. Along with the strawberry-tree (*arbutus*) liqueur, *Medronho*, and the bitter almond liqueur, *Amêndoa Amarga*, there are several good red Alentejo wines.

Handicrafts

Local handicrafts (*artesanato*) are well worth investigating both as souvenirs and for their practical value. The further you get away from the coast the better the quality is likely to be. In the Algarve, the town of Loulé is very much the centre of traditional craft skills, specialising particularly in copper and brass pots, including the unique Algarvian cooking utensil, the *cataplana*. Up in the mountains, the town of Monchique is also a good centre for handicrafts. For the best quality and design, look for small studios/shops of individual craftspeople, or artisans' cooperatives, such as the one in Beja, instead of the ubiquitous souvenir *artesanato* shops. In the latter, much of the merchandise is either mass-produced or imported – or both.

Leather

Leather articles are very good value, especially when bought in open markets. Loulé is once again the place to go for fancy goods, such as decorated bridles and saddles. Clothes are generally much cheaper than in other parts of Europe. For those looking for quality, the Rua Santa Isabel in Portimão has a number of stylish shops, as does the Rua Santo António in Faro.

Textiles

The distinctive Arraiolos carpets can be purchased in the Alentejo from the town of the same name and also from outlets in Évora (*Praça do Giraldo*) and in Portimão (*Rua Teofilo Braga*). The town of Mértola has a small cooperative that produces hand-woven woollen rugs and blankets in marvellously vibrant geometric patterns using the natural colours of the wool. Their workshop can be found down some steps opposite the tourist office in Rua da República.

Less spectacular, but considerably cheaper, are the locally woven striped rugs, found practically everywhere in the Algarve. Delicate crochet work was once a thriving cottage industry but it is now quite rare and tends to be pricey.

Delectable confections are available in every town

WHERE TO BUY
Western Algarve
Albufeira

Albufeira's principal shopping street is the pedestrianised Rua 5 de Outubro, close to the seafront.

Adega do Cantor
Producer of Sir Cliff Richard's Vida Nova wine. You might even spot the singer himself working away in the winery or vineyard. There are several tours a day and a shop selling the wine.
Quinta do Miradouro, Guia, 500m (550 yards) from Algarve Shopping Centre.
Tel: 968 776971.
www.winesvidanova.com.
Admission charge includes tasting.

Algarve Shopping Centre
Mega shopping mall with around 170 shops, hypermarket, multiplex cinema, bowling alley, restaurants and cafés. Children's facilities include a very reasonably priced crèche and free pushchairs and pedal cars.
On the N126 just outside Albufeira. Centre open: daily 9am–midnight; shops open: 10am–10pm.

Infante Dom Henrique
Large selection of porcelain, terracotta and crystal.
Rua Cándido dos Reis 30.
Tel: 289 513168.

Lagos

The town's centre has been pedestrianised.
Mundo do Sapato Huge shoe shop where popular brands are heavily discounted.
Loja Mestre Maco, on the N125, near Odiaxere, east of Lagos. Tel: 282 343065.
Opalina – Atelier
Beautifully hand-crafted jewellery and glass, along with regional handicrafts.
Praça do Infante 1.
Tel: 282 762121.

Portimão

There is a good selection of high-quality shops between Rua do Comércio and Rua Santa Isabel.
Porches Pottery Hand-painted regional pottery and Algarve handicrafts.
N125, Porches.
Tel: 282 381668.
Portimão Retail Park
Large new mall based around a vast hypermarket.

Chão das Donas, on the N125 between Portimão and Alvor junctions.

Praia da Rocha
Harmanna Exclusive
Designer and casual clothing, shoes and handbags.
Avenida Tomás Cabreira (opposite Hotel Algarve).
Tel: 282 423250.
And another branch at Rua do Comércio 33, Portimão.
Tel: 282 484986.

Sagres
Surf Planet Shop
Entirely devoted to surf gear, with the latest wetsuits, accessories and boards for all levels. Rental service is also available.
Estrada Nacional 268.
Tel: 282 624815.

Eastern Algarve
Faro

The capital of the Algarve has a good selection of shops centred around the pedestrianised Rua Santo António. There are also some interesting stores in the old part of town, near the cathedral.

Forum Algarve The largest and most attractively designed mall in the Algarve, featuring over 200 shops, a big hypermarket, multiplex cinema, restaurants and cafés.
N125 in the direction of the airport. Tel: 289 889300.
Vila Adentro Fascinating antique shop in the old town, selling ceramics, *azulejos*, woodcarvings and other *objets d'art.*
Largo Afonso III.
Tel: 289 821777.

Loulé
This quiet town is a good centre for crafts if you are prepared to shop around. The main shopping streets are the Rua 9 de Abril, by the pseudo-Moorish covered market, the pedestrianised Rua 5 de Outubro, and the Rua da Barbacã near the tourist office. The covered market itself is a good source of rustic earthenware plates and pots at very reasonable prices. Saturday morning is the best time to come.
Centro de Artesanato A wide variety of handmade rugs, earthenware jugs,

embroidered tablecloths, and *caraveis* (sailing ships) carved from wood.
Rua da Barbacã 11–13.
Tel: 289 415230.

Quinta do Lago
Quinta Shopping Centre
Upmarket mall at the entrance of the resort, with all manner of shops and restaurants. After a morning's shopping, you can choose from Chinese, Italian or French cuisine – or opt for an English pub!
Quinta do Lago.
Tel: 289 398247.

Lower Alentejo
Beja
ARABE (Associação Regional de Artesãos e Artistas de Beja) Inside the imposing portico of the old Misericórdia church is an excellent artisans' cooperative selling high-quality hand work in wood, leather, ceramic, sheep skin, cork and other media, including fur-lined woollen capes.
Praça da República.
Tel: 284 389545.
http://arabeja.com.sapo.pt

Upper Alentejo
Évora
The Alentejo is almost completely uncommer-cialised in comparison with the Algarve, but Évora has several very good craft shops in and around the main square, the Praça do Giraldo.
Luis Madeira For a rare chance to watch a skilled cork artist at work, find this tiny workshop where Luis Madeira carves (and sells) cork Christmas Nativity scenes.
Rua Mouraria (off Largo São Mamede).
Miranda Ferrão Watches and jewellery, including local filigree work.
Rua Mercadores 106.
Tel: 266 701386.
Nazareth & Filho Lda Stationery on the ground floor; books (including several about the region) on the first floor.
Praça do Giraldo 46.
Tel: 266 702221.
Oficina da Terra World-renowned terracotta sculpture workshop, gallery and shop.
Travessa Sertório 26.
Tel: 266 746049.
www.oficinadaterra.com

MARKETS

Shopping in covered food markets, or at street stalls in the open air, is a great way to experience the hustle and bustle of Portuguese life at first hand. In the covered food markets, traders are in direct competition with each other and call out encouragingly to the passing customers. If you want to eat really cheaply, there is no better way than by purchasing the ingredients for a picnic as you wander through. Home-made produce, such as cheeses and honey, can usually be purchased more cheaply than in shops and is often fresher. The buildings themselves are often architecturally interesting, notably the mock-Moorish market at Loulé. Outdoor markets vary from the lavish fairs that are set up especially for festivals and holidays to the regular markets that occur on a weekly or fortnightly basis. In both, there is always a wide variety of goods on offer from food and clothes to pottery and cassette tapes. Vendors are eager to sell, so this is where you will get the best bargains especially if you try haggling. Times can vary throughout the year so it is worth checking with the local tourist office. Look out also for fruit sellers who set up their stalls alongside roads and at which you can purchase cheap watermelons, seasonal fruits and home-grown vegetables.

If you are staying at one of the coastal towns or villages, it is worthwhile getting up as early as 7am to witness the fishing catch being brought in and auctioned off at the wholesale fish market. Albufeira is probably the easiest place to see this, at the Fishermen's Beach in the old part of town. The sheer variety of fish, from the exotic to the fearsome, is astonishing.

Western Algarve

Albufeira

Apart from the fish market, there is an outdoor market on the first and third Tuesday of each month by the Orada chapel.

Alte

Third Thursday of each month.

Alvor

Second Tuesday of each month.

Lagos

A large outdoor market on the first Saturday of each month and special fairs in August, October and November.

Monchique

Second Friday of each month.

Hand-crafted leather at bargain prices

Paderne (near Albufeira)
First Saturday of each month.

Portimão
First Monday of each month, at Caldeira do Moinho.

São Bartolomeu de Messines
Last Monday of each month.

São Marcos da Serra
First Saturday of each month.

Silves
Third Monday of each month.

Eastern Algarve
Estói (near Faro)
Second Sunday of each month.

Fuzeta (near Olhão)
First Thursday of each month.

Loulé
Every Saturday morning.

Moncarapacho (near Olhão)
First Sunday of each month.

Olhão
Covered markets for fish and for food next to each other on Avenida 5 de Outubro, fronting the Ria Formosa. Gypsy market first Sunday of each month.

Quarteira
Every Wednesday at Filipe Jonas Garden.

Terracotta pots for the garden

Tavira
Third Saturday of each month.

Vila Nova da Cacela
(near Vila Real de Santo António)
Third Sunday of each month.

Upper Alentejo
Évora
Second Tuesday of each month in the Rossio square near the Jardim Público (Public Gardens).

THE SPICE ROUTE

Until Vasco da Gama charted a major sea route between Portugal and India, via the Cape of Good Hope, the spice trade was monopolised by the Arabs. It was in July 1497 that this intrepid seaman set sail from Portugal, and arrived ten months later in Calicut in southwest India. Da Gama returned to Lisbon in 1499 in triumph and joined the ranks of the nobility.

A year later, Pedro Álvares Cabral was sent to set up colonies in India. Spices began to flow by sea to Europe, but many of his men were subsequently massacred by Arab merchants. Vasco da Gama was sent back to India to show the Arabs who was boss, taking savage revenge. In 1503, loaded with booty, he returned to Portugal, but he was soon to make the long voyage to India again, this time as Portuguese Viceroy. Shortly after his arrival, however, he fell ill and died.

Entertainment

There is no shortage of entertainment to be found in the Algarve, from visiting a cabaret to dancing the night away. On the whole, lowbrow activities tend to outnumber highbrow ones, but it does not all have to be mindless fun. During the summer months, several music festivals are mounted which often feature artists of international renown. In recent years, a number of art galleries have sprung up which display work by both contemporary Portuguese artists and foreigners.

Tourist offices are always the best source of information about local events, many of which are only publicised at short notice. The larger hotels also give out information and the fortnightly *Algarve News* is useful for listings, as is the monthly *Essential Algarve*. In Portimão, an occasional free information magazine, *Discover Portimão*, has listings; it can be found at the tourist office.

ART GALLERIES

Apart from a few big names, contemporary Portuguese art is practically unknown outside of Portugal.

But there is a thriving art scene and several interesting galleries deal in a wide range of work, from experimental to traditional.

Almancil

Centro Cultural São Lourenço
Temporary art exhibitions, and sculpture on the terraces and in the gardens.

Praça São Lourenço. Tel: 289 395475. www.centroculturalsaolourenco.com

Galeria da ASCA (Associação Social e Cultural de Almancil)
Temporary art exhibits.
Rua do Centro Comunitário.
Tel: 289 399699. www.asca.pt

Panda Art Gallery
The works of art are for sale as well as for viewing.
Rua Escanxinas. Tel: 289 395754.

Beja

Galeria Escudeiros
Temporary exhibits by Portuguese artists.
Rua dos Escudeiros 30. Tel: 284 311910.

Évora

Galeria Évora-Arte
Exhibits of known and young artists.
Rua Manuel do Olival 22. Tel: 266 701898.

Faro

Galeria de Arte Arco
Views of the Ria Formosa add to the

best contemporary Portuguese art.
Rua do Arco. Tel: 289 801037.

Galeria Municipal Trem
Contemporary art, both Portuguese
and foreign, shown in the company of a
Roman arch.
Rua do Trem 5. Tel: 289 804197.

Loulé
Galeria de Arte Convento Espírito Santo
Regularly scheduled exhibitions of
painting and sculpture by national and
foreign artists.
*Rua Vice Almirante Cândido Reis.
Tel: 289 313275.*

Portimão
EMARP Gallery
Changing exhibitions of contemporary
paintings, sculpture and photography.
*Rua José António Marques 17.
Tel: 282 400260. www.emarp.pt*

Tavira
Casa das Artes
Contemporary art, photography and
installations.
*Rua João Vaz Corte-Real 96. Tel:
281 322635. www.acasadasartes.com*

DISCOS AND NIGHTCLUBS
Nightclubs are to be found throughout
southern Portugal. In the Algarvian
resorts, they vie with each other to attract
custom with ever-more sensational
gimmicks. Things do not really start to
happen until 1am but they can then
continue until dawn. Entry prices at the
height of the tourist season can be high.

Albufeira
Crazy Bull Dancing
Dancing, DJs, live music and
performance, drag shows.
*Praça de Touros. Tel: 289 244070.
Open: 10pm–6am.*

Discoteca Bar Capítulo V
Popular nightspot with a largely
Portuguese crowd; offers its own
parking area.
Ed. Borda de Água. Tel: 289 586800.

Kiss
Biggest, most frenetic club in the area.
*Areias de São João. Tel: 289 590280.
Open: usually until 6am.*

Aljezur
Discoteca Monte de Mouro
Music and dancing.
Estr. Nacional 120. Tel: 282 947466.

Beja
Praxis
Disco; popular dancing spot for locals.
*Rua do Doutor Simões Bravo 1.
Tel: 284 325000.*

Carvoeiro
Jailhouse Carvoeiro
Live music or historic music videos,
dancing; popular since the '60s.
*Rua do Escondidinho. Tel: 282 357897.
www.carvoeiro.com/jailhouse*

Évora
Praxis Club
Disco and live music, dancing Wed–Sat.
*Rua de Valdevinos 21.
Tel: 266 708177. www.praxisclub.com*

Faro

In addition to being a tourist town, Faro is also a university town, so nightlife can be active. It tends to congregate mostly along Rua do Prior, Rua Conselheiro Bivar and Rua Infante Dom Henrique. Cafés are open most of the day and into the night; bars and clubs open later, usually starting at 9pm.

Bar do Conservatorio Regional do Algarve

Bar of the dance conservatory; check with them for performances.
Rua Dr Almeida Carrapato 93.
Tel: 289 873888.

Bar Upa Upa

Popular bar; the crowd spills out into the patio in warm weather.
Rua Conselheiro Bívar 51. Tel: 289 807832.

A *fadista* sings her tales of heartbreak

Dux
Disco club that has general appeal to locals and visitors.
Rua do Prior. Tel: 289 803601.

Lagos
Bon Vivant
Busy disco on four levels with a different vibe on each.
Rua 25 de Abril. Open: until 6am.
Le Privé
Fashionable place to dance.
Praia de Luz. Tel: 282 789100.
Praia de Rocha Katedral
Gargantuan disco on the front with terrace overlooking the sea.
Av. Tomás Cabreira. Tel: 282 424335.

Sagres
Mitic Cocktail Bar
Café and bar open all day and into the night, when they have either DJ or live music.
Av. Comandante Matoso.
Tel: 964 139350.

Vilamoura
Kadoc Disco
The largest nightclub in the Algarve, accommodating 7,000 or so on five floors. Foam parties on Sunday nights in summer, with house, electro, tech-house. Free bus from Faro and resorts.
On the N125 at Boliqueime.
Tel: 289 360485. www.kadoc.pt

CASINOS
For those with money to throw away, the Algarve has several casinos, which are open from 5pm until 4am. There is usually an entrance fee, passports or ID cards must be carried and men are required to wear jackets. Roulette, blackjack and baccarat are played and there are slot machines. There are also bars, restaurants and live entertainment on the premises; these can vary in quality but are consistently expensive. For info on any of the following casinos, visit
www.solverde.pt
Casino de Monte Gordo
Monte Gordo. Tel: 281 512261.
Casino de Vilamoura
Vilamoura. Tel: 289 302995.
Hotel Algarve Casino
Praia da Rocha, Portimão.
Tel: 282 415229.

FADO BARS
The melancholy songs of the *fado* are associated with Lisbon and Coimbra rather than the south of Portugal, but, rather like flamenco in Spain, its tourist appeal is such that *fado* clubs have sprung up everywhere. Unfortunately, performers can vary dramatically in standard. Various hotels and restaurants have *Fado* Nights, as do some local cultural centres; ask at the tourist office or your hotel.

Albufeira
Atrium
Fado accompanies dinner three evenings a week.
Rua 5 de Outubro 20.
Tel: 289 515755.

Lagos
Centro Cultural
Frequent *fado* concerts, along with other music styles.
Rua Lançarote de Freitas 7.
Tel: 282 770450.

Quarteira
Dallas Restaurant
Fado on Saturday evenings from 8pm.
Avenida Francisco Sa Carneiro.
Tel: 289 313818.

FILMS
Most foreign films are shown with their original soundtrack and Portuguese subtitles, although this is not always the case; it is a good idea to check first. Blockbuster films are shown here soon after release, and all major Algarve resorts have cinemas, often in the major shopping centres. Prices tend to be inexpensive. Larger towns in the Alentejo have cinemas, often in theatres that also host live performances.

Albufeira
Guia Castello Lopes
Nine-screen cinema showing original-soundtrack films.
Tavagueira Guia, Estrada Nacional 125.
Tel: 289 560351.
www.castellolopescinemas.com

Beja
Cine-Teatro
Largo de São João.
Tel: 284 315090.

Faro
Cinema Santo António
25 Rua Santo António.
Tel: 289 801350.

Portimão
Cinema de Portimão
Shows films in original languages with Portuguese subtitles.
Avenida Miguel Bombarda.
Tel: 282 411931.

Praia da Luz
Cine Estúdio
English- and Portuguese-language films.
Edifício Luztur. Tel: 282 703332.

Quartiera
Vilamoura Cine
Shows original-soundtrack films.
Largo das Estrelas.
Tel: 289 302377.

FOLK MUSIC AND DANCING
Southern Portugal has a strong indigenous music and dancing tradition, and, in recent years, many traditional local customs have been revived for tourist consumption. This can mean that, like shopping for handicrafts, you will come across the good, the bad and the indifferent. Many resorts organise folk-dancing displays in the summer evenings, and September is the month of the National Folklore Festival. In Faro, displays of folk dancing are given by the Rancho Folclórico de Faro. The village of Alte also has regular displays at the

Fonte Pequena Folklore Centre. During the summer in Albufeira, there is dancing almost every night in the Largo Eng Duarte Pacheco, starting at 10pm.

MUSIC

Apart from folk music and *fado* there are many other kinds of music to be found in the south. During May and June, there is an Algarve Music Festival which is predominantly classical and involves both Portuguese and foreign artists. Events are held in venues right across the Algarve. Look out for listings in churches of organ recitals and choral concerts. Recorded rock music is impossible to avoid, but major rock stars also perform live in the Algarve.

THEATRE AND PERFORMANCE VENUES

Although stage plays are almost always in Portuguese, theatres often host ballet, folkloric and musical programmes.

Almancil
Cultural Centre São Lourenço
Concerts of classical and jazz music.
Tel: 289 395475.
www.centroculturalsaolourenco.com

Évora
An active programme of events is held in numerous locations around the city. A free monthly *Agenda Cultural* is available at the tourist office (make sure you are picking up the right month).

Faro
Teatro das Figuras e Solar do Capitão-mor
The city's newest performance and event centre.
Horta das Figuras, Estrada Nacional 125.
Tel: 289 888100.
www.teatromunicipaldefaro.pt
Teatro Lethes
Performances in a fully restored opera house.
Rua de Portugal 59. Tel: 289 820300.
www.teatromunicipaldefaro.pt

Regional costumes at a festival in Belem

Music and dance

The most moving and powerful music to be heard in the south is the three-part male-voice singing of the Alentejo. Melancholy, slow and regular, the songs tell of the struggles of the land and the pain of death. A single voice intones the verse and is joined by the other voices in the chorus, the absence of any other accompaniment intensifying the rawness of the emotion. This type of singing is strongest in the Serpa district and around the village of Cuba.

In the Algarve, there is more enthusiasm for dancing than for singing. The best known of the region's dances is the *corridinho*, a kind of circular polka danced in pairs with much whirling of skirts and stamping of feet.

In Pechão, near Olhão, the traditional 'Dance of the Moors'

Azulejos with a *fado* theme

A holiday or festive event is an occasion to dress up, even for children

used to be performed in September. This was similar to the Mouriscas (battle dances between Christians and Moors) found throughout the Iberian peninsula. These dances are now best seen at local fairs and festivals, but they are also performed at organised folklore events and centres, such as the Fonte Pequena Folklore Centre, in the village of Alte, and at the Hotel Eva in Faro.

Fado has become so closely identified with Portugal, through the fame of its greatest exponent, Amália Rodrigues, that fado bars have appeared on the south coast. These gloomy ballads of love and death, accompanied by the plaintive Portuguese guitar, were originally from, and exclusive to, Lisbon. There are regular performances of fado at the Hotel Eva in Faro and at the Sol e Mar Hotel in Albufeira.

Children

Activities for children and teens centre around the beaches and resorts of the Algarve, more than in the Alentejo. At the beaches are pedalos and windsurfing (equipment and lessons are available at Praia da Luz and many other beaches) and the larger resort hotels organise programmes for children.

But in the midst of all these beach activities are places where young visitors can also delight in the local culture and history. There are castle ramparts to guard, and Roman ruins where imaginations can run wild, not to mention wonderfully creepy bone chapels. There are very few facilities, children's museums or theatres. Bored teenagers looking for action away from the beach are well served by such delights as snooker halls, mini-golf, bowling alleys and even video arcades in the larger resorts along the Algarve coast.

Several entertainment centres are primarily aimed at children, the most popular of which are the water parks, zoos and amusement parks that line the N125 across the Algarve.

Riding lessons are widely available (*see* Sport and leisure, *p154*).

Water parks and zoos

Most water parks open in early June and close by mid-September, and are open from 9am or 10am to 6pm or 7pm.

Aqualand
Europe's biggest open-air water park with swimming pool with waves and water chutes.
N125, Alcantarilha. Tel: 282 322827.
www.aqualand.pt

Aquashow
Water park and full-scale amusement park with roller coasters and more.
Quarteira. Tel: 289 389396.
www.aquashowpark.com

Slide & Splash
More aquatic entertainment with water chutes and slides.
N125 at Vale de Deus, Estômbar.
Tel: 282 340800. www.slidesplash.com

Zoolagos – Parque Zoológico de Lagos
More than 140 species of animals, plenty for the whole family.
Quinta das Figueiras,
Barão de São João. Tel: 282 680100.
www.zoolagos.com

Mini-golf courses

Mini-Golfe das Açoteias
A complete 18-hole course.
Turístico Aldeias de Açoteias,
Albufeira.

Mini-Golfe Dom Pedro
One of several sporting facilities.
Hotel Dom Pedro,
Vilamoura.
Tel: 289 300780.

Mini-Golfe Hotel Algarve
Full course.
Praia da Rocha, Portimão.
Tel: 282 235001.

For watersports and all other sports, *see*
pp150–57.

Castles
Silves and Marvão each have one of
Iberia's most appealing castles, with
ramparts to guard and passages to
explore. Throughout the Alentejo are
other castles where children can relive
the days of knights and fair princesses,
some in various states of romantic
decay, others quite well preserved or
restored. Beja, Serpa and Castelo de
Vide are good choices, and in the
Algarve there are also castles at Tavira
and Castro Marim.

Making waves at Quarteira's Aquashow

Castelo de Vide

A tiny village hides inside the castle walls, and you can climb the keep for an archer's-eye view down on the rooftops of the town (*see p115*).
Open: daily Jun–Sept 9am–7pm; Oct–May 9am–5pm.

Marvão

The entire town is enclosed by walls, and at the far end a magnificent castle overlooks Spain, its towers and ramparts intact. Be sure to see the giant oven, to the right inside the gate (*see p116*).
Open: daily until late evening.

Sagres

At the windswept point of Prince Henry the Navigator's headquarters (*see pp28–33*), there is no escaping the feeling that you are really standing at the end of the earth, as people believed before the Age of Discovery. There's not a lot to see, but the place itself will make the feats of the great explorers seem more real to children as they learn about them in school.

Silves

Allow plenty of time to circle the ramparts, and be sure to climb down into the vast cistern of this Moorish stronghold (*see p45 & pp48–9*).
Open: daily Sept–Jun 9am–5pm; Jul–Aug 9am–8pm.

Bone chapels

Kids love spooky things, and there's nothing much creepier than an entire room decorated in patterns formed by human skulls and bones. Intended to impart a message of the fleeting nature of life, there are several of these, but the easiest to access are at Évora's São Francisco church (*see p102*) and the Igreja do Carmo in Faro (*see p58*). Follow signs to 'Capela dos Ossos'.

Roman sites

Even fairly young schoolchildren have heard of the Romans, and the ruins of their cities are unaccountably fascinating to them. One of Portugal's finest is unearthed in the Upper Alentejo, at Miróbriga (*see pp96–7*). But there are smaller sites in both the Algarve and the Alentejo that are also worth visiting.

Ammaia

A Roman city slowly emerges – a good place for older children to see an archaeological dig in progress.
Portagem, below Marvão. Open: daily 9am–12.30pm & 2–5.30pm.

Milreu

The extensive villa is especially interesting for its baths, and to see how a later farmhouse was built on top of it.
Open: Tue–Sun 9.30am–12.30pm & 2–5pm.

Miróbriga

The 25,000-seat amphitheatre and baths, where the system for heating and circulating water is clearly visible, give a picture of Roman life. Let children

São Francisco in Évora – one of the so-called bone chapels

wonder (along with the archaeologists) what treasures are still buried in the unexcavated parts.

Santiago do Cacém. Open: Tue–Sat 9am–noon & 2–5.30pm.

Food and accommodation

Restaurants are used to catering for children since the Portuguese tend to include their children in all social events. Several have special menus, but even if they don't, it is easy to find simple food. A child under eight years of age sharing a hotel room with his parents is entitled to a 50 per cent discount, and many hotels will make arrangements for babysitting.

Sport and leisure

Southern Portugal is a paradise for sports enthusiasts. Rain is infrequent, the many beaches are ideal for watersports, there is a fine marina at Vilamoura, and the Algarve boasts some of Europe's most outstanding golf courses. The midday sun can be oppressive at the height of the summer, even with the Atlantic breezes, but many facilities stay open into the evening so it is possible to avoid the hottest times.

Fishing

It is possible to hire equipment for fishing offshore or in the large inland reservoirs.

The big attraction of the Atlantic coast, however, is the potential for deep-sea or big-game fishing. This is expensive but increasingly popular.

Over 200 species of fish swim in these waters; the more spectacular include tuna, blue and mako shark, swordfish, bass, marlin, ray and conger eel. Previous experience is not necessary, though anyone prone to seasickness should be cautious; the waters are calm in summer but can be rough in winter, the optimum time for fishing. Praia da Rocha and Vilamoura are the main centres and there are different rates for fishermen and spectators.

Big Game Fishing

A 13m (43ft) long boat, the *Sant' Anna*, does a whole day's cruise. Lunch must be ordered in advance.

Algarve Seafaris, Quai C,
Marina da Vilamoura.
Tel: 289 302318.
www.algarve-seafaris.com

Cepemar Big Game Fishing Centre

This is one of the most professional outfits and is run by Rudolf Streur. Cruises begin at 9am and lunch must be ordered in advance.

Portas da Rocha, lote 7, loja B,
Praia da Rocha. Tel: 282 425866.
www.biggamefishing.info

Golf

The attractions of golfing in the Algarve are numerous – the temperate climate, the beautiful surroundings and, above all, the quality of the courses, many of which are championship standard. For details on more than 30 major golf courses, visit *www.algarvegolf.net*

Unfortunately, some of the top clubs are so exclusive that getting a game is almost impossible and, if you manage it, extremely expensive.

Laguna & Millennium

Two American-designed courses with difficult water hazards.

Vilamoura. Tel: 289 310180/333.

www.oceanicogolf.com

Palmares

Designed by Frank Penninck, a par-71 course with fine views of the sea and of the distant mountains.

Lagos. Tel: 282 790500.

www.palmaresgolf.com

Parque de Floresta

A well-designed but difficult par-72 course set in hilly countryside.

Budens, 15km (9 miles) from Lagos.

Tel: 282 690054.

www.parquedafloresta.com

Penina

This par-73 Henry Cotton course is used for major tournaments.

Montes de Alvor, near Portimão.

Tel: 282 420200.

www.lemeridienpenina.com/pt/golfe

Pinhal

Various designers have had a hand in this course, so it is full of surprises.

Vilamoura. Tel: 289 310390.

www.oceanicogolf.com

Quinta do Lago

Designed by Bill Mitchell, this is an immaculately kept course which is heavily booked up and very expensive.

Almancil. Tel: 289 390700.

www.quintadolagogolf.com

Quinta da Ria

Newer course with a beautiful setting over the Ria Formosa.

Near Castro Marim.

Tel: 281 950580.

www.quintadariagolf.com

The Algarve has some of the world's best golf courses

Sport and leisure

São Lourenço

To get a game at this American-designed par-72 18-hole course, it helps to be staying at the Penina Hotel or the Hotel Dona Filipa.

Quinta do Lago. Tel: 289 396522.
www.quintaproperty.com

The Old Course Vilamoura

Set among pinewoods, the Penninck-designed course is one of Europe's best.

Tel: 289 310341. www.oceanicogolf.com

Vale do Lobo

Another Henry Cotton design, it has narrow fairways and a spectacular seventh hole on its Yellow Course which crosses two ravines.

Almancil. Tel: 289 390700.
www.valedolobo.com/golf

Spectator sports

Many Portuguese are keen sports fans and they support their teams with great enthusiasm. Football is a national obsession. There are no outstanding teams in the south, though there are professional league teams at Faro, Lagos, Portimão and Vila Real de Santo António. The atmosphere at a match is partisan but friendly; games are seen as family entertainment, and the occasional bad behaviour is castigated by officials as 'English' – clearly a synonym for unruliness.

Touradas

The Portuguese bullfight, or *tourada*, is less violent than the Spanish *corrida*,

Dramatic encounter in the bullring

Caravel cruise along the Algarve cliffs at Ferragudo

and great emphasis is placed on the skilled horsemanship of the *cavaleiro*. Dressed in ornate 18th-century-style costume, the *cavaleiro* has to place six *bandarillas*, or darts, into the bull's shoulders. Since 2001, it has been illegal to kill the bull at a fight in Portugal.

For those who take an interest, the best fights take place in the Ribatejo region and in Lisbon, but regular *touradas* are held in many parts of southern Portugal on Saturday evenings throughout the summer.

Boat trips

For a leisurely time on the water, there are many pleasure cruises available.
Bom Dia
Traditional Portuguese sailing ships that operate two-hour trips to the caves, half-day barbecue cruises in the Bay of Lagos

and three-hour family fishing trips.
Marina de Lagos, loja 10.
Tel: 282 087587.
www.bomdia-boattrips.com
Condor de Vilamoura
The *Condor de Vilamoura* is a tall ship which runs full- and half-day cruises along the Algarve coast.
Marina da Vilamoura. Tel: 289 314070.
Ecotourism Boat Tours
Pontoon boat tours of the Ria Formosa for views of the barrier islands, birdwatching and fishing history.
Olhão. Tel: 918 056674.
www.natura-algarve.com
Hobie Kayak
Tours of the Ria Formosa and its islands by pedal and sail-powered kayaks.
Ria Formosa. Tel: 966 034723.
www.hobiekayaks.co.uk
Santa Bernarda Caravel Cruises
Cruises from Portimão, along the coast

and to the sea caves on a two-masted caravel.

Cais Vasco da Gama (near the Naval Club of Portimão). Tel: 282 422791, 967 023840. www.santa-bernarda.com

Riding

There are many riding centres (Centros Hípicos) across the region, and most offer lessons to beginners.

Centro Hípico de Vilamoura

Stadium with jumps, cross-country riding and beach treks.

*Qta da Quarteira, Loulé.
Tel: 289 322675.*

Quinta dos Amigos

Treks along the coast and tuition for beginners.

*Almancil. Tel: 289 393399.
www.quintadosamigos.com*

Tiffany's Riding Centre

Lessons for children and beginners.

Vale Grifo 1677-E. Almadena, near Lagos. Tel: 282 697395.

Vale de Ferro Riding Centre

Scenic cross-country rides in the foothills of Monchique from well-equipped stables with 30 horses. Free pickup service from Lagos and Portimão. Jeep safaris on request.

*Mexilhoeira Grande, Portimão.
Tel: 282 968444.
www.algarvehorseholidays.com*

Watersports

The combination of south-facing beaches, warm weather and cool waters makes the Algarve a perfect location for watersports. The calmer waters of the southern strip of coast make it ideal for swimming, for snorkelling or for scuba

The Algarve offers perfect conditions for watersports for everyone, from experts to beginners

Surfing in Porto Batel

diving. The main resorts have lifeguards in attendance and a system of flags to indicate whether it is safe to swim. Green indicates safety, yellow means take care, and red is for danger. A blue checked flag shows that the lifeguard is no longer in attendance.

The Atlantic Ocean has a powerful undertow and even experienced swimmers should exercise caution.

Equipment for fishing from the shore, or from jetties, can be hired in many resorts. Rather more exciting is to go deep-sea fishing in search of bass, marlin and tuna, or even for shark. No experience is necessary, but a day's outing will be expensive. A more modest alternative is to try the local fishermen, who will sometimes take visitors out for a tour of the waters – whether for fishing or just for sightseeing.

There are many places from which to hire boats, both sailing dinghies and motorboats. Windsurfing and waterskiing are also increasingly popular. The western coast is something of a mecca for surfers, the beaches around the village of Carrapateira being especially fine. An alternative to the sea for sporting enthusiasts is the number of large inland reservoirs that exist in the south, many of which have facilities for sailing and windsurfing. However, be warned that in summer there can be a dramatic drop in the water level as the reservoirs shrink.

Check locally for horse-racing events

Algarve Windsurfing and Sailing Centre

Established in the 1980s, it provides equipment and expert instruction and is good for beginners of all ages. Also has equipment for waterskiing and sailing.

Praia Grande, Ferragudo. Tel: 282 461115.

Beach Hut Watersports

Boat trips, powerboat rentals, sailing, windsurfing, kayaks and more, on the beach.

Praia da Luz. Tel: 919 553476, 919 760773. www.beachhutwatersports.com

Freeride

Surf camp and school open to surfers of all levels. The action takes place near Sagres, on either the south or west coast, depending on wind and swell direction.

Casa Azul, Praça da República, Sagres. Tel: 916 089005.
www.freeridesurfcamp.com

Tennis

As well as the following tennis clubs, many hotels also have courts.

Performance Tennis School

Ten all-weather courts.

Carvoeiro. Tel: 282 357847.

Vale do Lobo Tennis

Prestigious academy with fourteen all-weather courts, including six which are floodlit.

Vale do Lobo. Tel: 289 357850.
www.valedolobo.com

Vilamoura Tennis Centre

Twelve courts, equipment hire, a pro shop, a bar and a restaurant plus expert tuition.

Vilamoura. Tel: 289 324123.
http://premier-sports.org

Hiking and cycling

Organised tours and bike rentals are more common in the Algarve than in the Alentejo. An excellent and inexpensive guide to walking, hiking and mountain-bike routes, *Planície Dourada Nature Trails*, is available at tourist offices in Serpa and the Lower Alentejo.

Alternativtour

Guided hiking, canoeing, rappelling and mountain-biking expeditions in the Serra de Monchique and Monte Foia.

Sitio das Relvinhas, Apartado 122, Monchique.
Tel: 282 913204, 965 004337.
www.alternativtour.com

Megasport Rent A Bike

Bicycle rentals of all sorts and guided bicycle tours.

N125 (Km 89), Quatro Estradas.
Tel: 289 393044. www.megasport.pt

Walkin' Sagres

Walks and hikes in the Natural Park of Southwest Alentejo and Costa Vicentina.

Ana Carla Cabrita, Sagres. Tel: 925 545515. www.walkinsagres.com

Sailing comes naturally to this land of legendary navigators

Food and drink

Eating out in Portugal can be a joy: the food is wholesome, it comes in large helpings and is usually inexpensive. There are many regional specialities but fish dominates the menu in the Algarve, while meats – especially the locally raised pork – have a slightly bigger share in the Alentejo. Boiled potatoes are normally served with fish, chips with grilled meats. Cooked green vegetables are uncommon (except in soups), side salads being more usual. Choices for vegetarians are improving gradually.

PORTUGUESE FOOD

Despite a wide variety of different regional dishes, the traveller in Portugal will find that a number of popular recipes feature on most menus. *Caldo verde*, for example, is a rich vegetable soup made from finely shredded kale that originated in the northern Minho region. *Bacalhau* (dried salted cod) is ubiquitous. The dishes you are most likely to find on the menu are *bacalhau à brás* (flaked with onions), *bacalhau à gomes de sá* (flaked with potatoes and hard-boiled eggs) and *bacalhau com nata* (flaked with cream).

The DOC (Designation of Origin) *Queijo Serpa* is an outstanding sheep's milk cheese from the Alentejo; either in its soft fresh form or aged, it goes well with Port wine.

Algarvian specialities

There is rather more to Algarvian cooking than grilled sardines and shellfish – delicious though these are. Many recipes are prepared using a *cataplana*, a round-bottomed pan with a similarly shaped lid attached by a hinge which preserves all the juices and flavour of *cataplana* dishes such as pork, *bacalhau* and clams. The Algarve has its own version of the refreshingly cold Spanish soup, *gazpacho*, which employs bread, peppers, cucumber and tomatoes. *Caldeirada*, a fish soup or stew, is also very popular.

Perhaps the region's greatest claim to culinary fame is its sweets and pastries. Figs and almonds, a legacy of Moorish times, feature strongly here. One of the best-known confections is *Dom Rodrigo*, a very sweet mixture of egg yolk and ground almonds wrapped in twists of silver paper. Another is the *morgado*, a sphere of glazed white sugar with a silver ball on top and a sweet almond paste inside.

Conventual sweets traditionally made by nuns in the Alentejo are now available in *pastelarias* everywhere.

These are often made with local almonds or filled with custard made from fresh cottage cheese. Each baker seems to have a special version.

Alentejan specialities

Açordas, made by soaking dry bread to produce a kind of soup that is then flavoured with coriander leaves and topped with poached eggs, is delicious. Local game dishes – stewed hare, roast partridge and grilled wild boar – are also particularly good. *Porco a Alentejana* is an appetising dish of marinated pork cooked with small freshwater clams. *Porco preto*, a local breed of pig, is especially tender and flavourful, and is designated on menus.

Typical ingredients

açúcar sugar
alho garlic
amêijoas clams
arroz rice
assado roast
atum tuna
azeitonas olives
bacalhau cod
bife steak (not always beef)
borrego lamb
cabrito kid
caça game
camarão/ões shrimp/s
caranguejo crab
carapau horse mackerel
carne meat
cavala mackerel
chouriço smoked sausage
coelho rabbit

costeletas chops
couve cabbage
feijão verde green bean
feijoada bean stew
fiambre ham
figo fig
frango chicken
frutas fruit
gambas prawns
gelado ice cream
laranja orange
leitão suckling pig
limão lemon
linguado sole
lulas squid
maçã apple
manteiga butter
mariscos shellfish
melão melon
mexilhões mussels
molho sauce
morangos strawberries
ostra oyster
ovo egg
pão bread
pargo bream
peixes fish
pescada hake
pescadinha whiting
pêssego peach
presunto smoked ham
queijos cheese
robalo bass
salada verde/mista green/mixed salad
salmonete red mullet
torrada toast
uvas grapes
vaca beef
vitela veal

Food and drink

Food and drink

The vineyards of the Algarve

PORTUGUESE WINES AND DRINKS

The Algarve produces few wines, but those from the Alentejo (*see pp168–9*) are usually found on menus, along with those from elsewhere in Portugal. A good white wine with lunch or in the summer heat is Vinho Verde, a light and slightly sparkling wine made in the north from young grapes, hence the *verde* (green) in its name. Its alcohol content is fairly low.

The well-known Algarvian liqueur, the powerful *medronho*, is made from the strawberry-like berries of the *Arbutus unedo* tree. Other liqueurs use almonds (*amarguinha*) and honey (*brandymel*).

Port, the drink most associated with Portugal, is also produced in the north – along the valley of the Douro River. It is a dessert wine that has been fortified with grape spirit. Ruby port is young, full-bodied and sweet; tawny port, aged for longer, is less sweet and more delicate in taste; white port is an aperitif, and best drunk chilled.

Non-alcoholic drinks

Coffee drinking is a serious pastime for the Portuguese and there are several different ways of serving it.

A small black coffee, like an espresso, is called *uma bica*, and a small white coffee is *um garoto*. A larger cup of coffee made with milk is known as *uma meia de leite*, and a tumbler full of frothed-up milk with a small coffee added is called *um galão*. If you want your *bica* diluted ask for *uma bica cheia*, and for a slightly milkier *galão* ask for *um galão de máquina*. For American-style coffee, ask for *abatanado*. Decaffeinated coffee is *decafenado*, increasingly available.

Portugal has many springs and spas and a wealth of bottled mineral waters.

Your *água mineral* can come *com gas* (sparkling) or *sem gas* (still), and its temperature can be either *fresco* (cool) or *natural* (room temperature). Most of the spas are north of Lisbon, but Caldas de Monchique in the Algarve produces a particularly healthy and refreshing water.

WHERE TO EAT

In the main resorts restaurants can stay open late, but in the country it is not unusual for them to close by 9pm. The busiest time for dinner is 8pm. Lunch can begin as early as 12.30pm and it can be difficult to order much later than 2pm. It is advisable to telephone in advance to check opening times, to make a reservation and ask for more detailed instructions on how to get there.

There is a wide range of prices and it is easy to eat out well for very little money, although this is becoming increasingly difficult in the more touristy areas. Portions tend to be large and it is possible for two people to share a main dish (*uma dose*) or simply to have a half portion (*uma meia dose*) per person. A selection of starters – ranging from a bowl of olives to elaborate dishes – may be brought to the table, but you pay only for those you eat. If you don't sample them, they are removed.

In the following list of recommended restaurants, the star rating indicates the approximate cost in euros of a two-course meal per person, with coffee and a beer or half a bottle of house wine (shellfish – *mariscos* – are always more expensive).

★	under €25
★★	€25–40
★★★	€40–55
★★★★	over €55

Food and drink

Eminently drinkable Portuguese wines

Western Algarve

Albufeira

Paulu's Pizzeria ★
The pizzas and pastas here are popular with families and there are children's menus. Take-away available.
Edifício Oura Claudios, Estrada da Santa Eulália.
Tel: 289 587159.

A Ruina ★★★
This well-known building is on Fishermen's Beach. Several floors, fresh seafood, unpretentious.
Rua Cais Herculano.
Tel: 289 512094. www. restaurante-ruina.com

Cabaz da Praia ★★★
Cliffside terrace with a fine sea view. Varied cuisine.
Praça Miguel Bombarda.
Tel: 289 512137.

Restaurante do Hotel Vila Joya ★★★★
The exquisite dishes of this mega-elegant restaurant have earned it two Michelin stars. Reservations for non-hotel guests are essential.
Hotel Vila Joya, Praia de Galé.
Tel: 289 591795.
www.vilajoya.com

Aljezur

Pont' a Pé ★★
Overlooking a shady little riverside park, this cheery restaurant serves grilled fresh fish and *porco preto*, the locally raised pork.
Largo da Liberdade.
Tel: 282 998104.

Carvoeiro

Casa Velha do Pescador ★★★
In an old fisherman's cottage overlooking the beach, serving African-style prawns, shellfish *cataplana*, lamb shank, wild boar and vegetarian dishes.
Praia de Benagil, 3km (2 miles) east of Carvoeiro.
Tel: 282 358840.
Closed: Sat.

O Rústico ★★★
Traditional restaurant with charcoal grills and fish.
Caramujeira.
Tel: 282 342933.

Guia

O Teodósio ★
Also known as Rei dos Frangos (King of the Chickens), this is a huge noisy restaurant with communal tables renowned for chicken *piri-piri*. Be prepared to queue.
Rua do Emigrante 50, Estrada de Algoz.
Tel: 289 561318.

Lagos

A Floresta ★★
Well-prepared local meat and seafood specialities in a congenial atmosphere.
Rua António Chrisógono dos Santos 51.
Tel: 282 763719.

Jota 13 ★★
Popular for its grilled seafood.
Rua 25 Abril 58.
Tel: 282 762319.

O Galeão ★★★
Good international cuisine in a lively atmosphere.
Rua da Laranjeira 1.
Tel: 282 763909.

A Lagosteira ★★★
A favourite for seafood, especially the fish *cataplana*.
Rua 1 de Maio 20.
Tel: 282 762486.

Monchique

Bica-Boa ★★
Luxuriant surroundings, good and varied cuisine.
Estrada de Lisboa 266.
Tel: 282 912271.

A Charrete ★★
Friendly local restaurant with reasonably priced tourist menu.
Rua Dr Jamora Gil 30.
Tel: 282 912142.
Closed: Wed.

Paraiso da Montanha ★★★
Regional cooking; chicken *piri-piri* is the speciality.
3km (2 miles) from Monchique on the Fóia road. Tel: 282 912150.

Paderne
Veneza ★
Modest roadside restaurant serving *cataplana*, fig and almond desserts and other Algarvian fare.
On the road to Albufeira.
Tel: 289 367129.

Porches
O Leão ★★★★
Restored 17th-century farmhouse with garden; international cuisine.
Rua da Igreja.
Tel: 282 381384.
Dinner only.

Portimão
Casa Inglesa ★
Sit in the café outside for a roast pork sandwich or at a table inside for a meal. Be sure to step inside to look at the cases of tempting pastries, for which they are famous.
Praça Manuel Texeira Gomes 2.
Tel: 282 416290.
www.casainglesa.com

Pavilhão Snack Bar ★
Vegetarian snacks and small meals.

Avenida Miguel Bombarda.
Tel: 282 416512.

Mariners ★★
Restaurant and pub in a fine 18th-century building. Good-value international cuisine and special children's menu.
Rua Santa Isabel 28.
Tel: 282 425848.

O Buque ★★★
Large interior; specialising in *cataplana* dishes.
Parchal, near the Ferragudo side of the bridge.
Tel: 282 424678.

Dona Barca ★★★
This restaurant specialises in fish dishes and Algarvian desserts.
Largo da Barca.
Tel: 282 248189.

A Lanterna ★★★
Specialising in seafood, especially smoked swordfish and fish soup.
Near the old Portimão bridge. Tel: 282 414429.
Closed: Sun.

Praia da Rocha
La Dolce Vita ★★
Popular pizzeria across the main road from the beach. Choice of 26

A tasty street snack in Portimão

pizzas and home-made pasta; takeaway available.

Avenida Tomás Cabreira, opposite the Hotel Algarve Casino.

Tel: 282 419444.

Churrasqueira da Rocha ★★★

Beach-view restaurant specialising in grilled meats and chicken *piri-piri.*

Avenida Tomás Cabreira.

Tel: 282 417452.

Sagres

Bistro Bar Dromedario ★

Light meals and snacks in an upbeat setting. A good selection of pizzas, salads, sandwiches and crêpes. *Batidos,* milkshakes made with fresh fruit, are their speciality.

Avenida Comandante Matoso. Tel: 282 624219. www.dromedariosagres. com

A Tasca ★★

Excellent seafood and good views of the harbour.

Porto de Sagres.

Tel: 282 624177.

Memmo Restaurante ★★★

The Memmo is an attractive modern dining room with views over the

harbour at Sagres. Its menu is Mediterranean with an emphasis on quality local produce.

Memmo Baleeira Hotel, Sitio Baleeira.

Tel: 282 624212.

Silves

Café Inglês ★

English-run café/ restaurant behind the cathedral. Delicious home-made cakes and traditional Portuguese fare.

Escadas do Castelo 11.

Tel: 282 442585.

Rui Marisqueira ★★★

Justifiably renowned as one of the top seafood restaurants in the Algarve. Hugely popular so book in advance or be prepared to queue.

Rua Comendador Vilarinho 32.

Tel: 282 442682.

Eastern Algarve

Almancil

Restaurant Adega Cova ★★

Good country cooking with kid a speciality.

Vale de Eguas.

Tel: 289 395281.

Pequeno Mundo ★★★★

Gourmet French cuisine within a beautifully

converted farmhouse. Dinner only.

Tel: 289 399866. www. restaurantepequenomundo. com

Vincent Nas ★★★★

A 19th-century farmhouse specialising in French cuisine.

Estrada da Fonte Santa, Escanxinas (Almancil–Quarteira road).

Tel: 289 399093.

Dinner only, Tue–Sat.

Estói

Monte do Casal ★★★★

If you can afford only one splurge, it should be here, for either a five-course degustation menu or a dinner from the regular menu. Each dish is a work of art, as pleasing to the eye as to the palate, from the first bite of seafood Bernaise wrapped in house-smoked salmon.

Cerro do Lobo.

Tel: 289 990140.

www.montedocasal.pt

Faro

Adega Nova ★

Large and bustling marine-themed restaurant with communal tables. Sizzling fish and meat dishes are

served with jugs of wine.
Rua Francisco Barreto 24.
Tel: 289 813433.

O Barao ★
Tiny, friendly and
handily located a few
steps from the Arco da
Vila, there are no better
grilled sardines in Faro
than in this plain little
dining room. Prawns in
garlic or fresh tuna steak
are equally good.
Rua Albergue 16.
Tel: 289 823920.

Bella Italia ★★
Pizza and pasta dishes.
Rua Dr Francisco Gomes
10. Tel: 289 821978.
www.bellaitalia.pt

Mesa dos Mouros ★★
Rustic restaurant in the
shadow of Faro's
cathedral. Wild boar
is a speciality.
Largo da Sé 10.
Tel: 289 878873. Closed:
Sat lunch & Sun.

Camané ★★★
Upmarket beach
restaurant renowned
for seafood.
Avenida Nascente, Praia
de Faro. Tel: 289 817539.

Clube Naval ★★★
Harbour restaurant
specialising in fish dishes.
Doca de Faro.
Tel: 289 823434.

Dois Irmãos ★★★
Long-established
restaurant serving
excellent local cuisine.
Largo do Terreiro do
Bispo 13–14.
Tel: 289 823337.

Moncarapacho
Maragota's ★★
Overlooking the Colina
Verde golf course near
Olhão. Regional cuisine
with a contemporary twist.
Sitio da Maragota.
Tel: 289 790117.

Quarteira
Adega do Peixe ★★
Spacious restaurant with
a good view, well known
for its varieties of fresh
seafood.
Avenida Infante de Sagres.
Tel: 289 388370.

Tavira
Beira Rio Bars and
Restaurants ★★
Restaurants, bars and
a snooker room in a
warehouse overlooking
the river. Noted for its
garlic-flavoured quails.
Rua Borda d'Água da
Asseca 40.
Tel: 281 323165.
www.beirariotavira.com.
Closed: Sun evening.

Bica ★★
The friendly staff will
cook dishes to your taste.
Rua Almirante Cándido
dos Reis 22–24.
Tel: 281 323843.

Quatro Águas ★★
One of a cluster of fish
restaurants near the river
port, with fine views of
the lagoon.
Sítio das Quatro Águas.
Tel: 281 325329.

Ponto de Encontro ★★★
A restaurant with a good
selection of regional
dishes.
Praça Dr António
Padinha 39.
Tel: 281 323730.

Vilamoura
Pier One ★★★
Book a table on the
terrace and enjoy the
views of Vilamoura's
marina. International
cuisine.
Cais da Esperança
Clube Naútico.
Tel: 289 322734.

Vila Real de Santo
António
Caves do Guadiana ★★
Good for seafood,
Portuguese style.
Avenida da República 89.
Tel: 281 544498.

Food and drink

Lower Alentejo
Beja
Restaurante Luís de Rocha ★★★
An old restaurant situated near the tourist office. One of its specialities is traditional Alentejan pork dishes.
Rua Capitão João Francisco de Sousa 63.
Tel: 284 323179.
www.luizdarocha.com

Castro Verde
Restaurante Castro ★
The smart upstairs dining room overlooks the main street through a solid wall of windows that open in the summer. Order local pork (*porco preto*) or *plumas* (a fork-tender and delicious beefsteak).
Rua Fialho de Almeida 1.
Tel: 286 322614.
Closed: Sun.

Serpa
Dom Luis ★
For a snack or a light lunch, ask for a plate of *enchidos*, and savour a selection of locally made sausages, ham and salami. These and other gourmet foods are also sold in the shop, along with fine Alentejo wines.
Praça da República 15.
O Cuiça ★★
Cool interior; good, reasonably priced Alentejan fare.
Rua das Portas de Beja 18.
Tel: 284 549566.

Vila Nova de Milfontes
A Fateixa ★
Very simple restaurant serving generous, simple dishes on a terrace overlooking the bay. The fish is impeccably fresh.
Largo do Cais.
Tel: 283 996415.

Water from Caldas de Monchique

Upper Alentejo
Estremoz
Pastelaria Formosa ★
The speciality of this bakery café is *guizos*, delectable little almond-filled tarts.
Rossio do Marquês de Pombal 93.
Tel: 268 339332.
Aguias d'Ouro ★★★
Good restaurant in the town's main square, and also near the tourist office.
Rossio do Marquês de Pombal 27.
Tel: 268 339100.
Pousada da Rainha Santa Isabel ★★★★
One of the most attractive *pousadas* in Portugal with a wonderful location overlooking the town. Has a high reputation for comfort and excellent local cuisine. Reservations are essential.
Largo de Dom Dinis.
Tel: 268 332075.

Évora
A Muralha ★
Unpretentious café just off the main square.
Rua 5 de Outubro 21.
Tel: 266 702284.
Closed Sun.

Pane & Vino ★★

Lively pizzeria; popular and charming.

Pateo do Salema 22.
Tel: 266 746960.

O Antão ★★★

Good new restaurant serving local cuisine and exhibiting the work of local painters.

Rua João de Deus 5–7.
Tel: 266 706459.
www.antao.pt

O Trovador ★★★

Busy, atmospheric and cordial, this restaurant tucked away in a side street is well known locally for its exceptional starters of cured meats and shellfish; these are brought to the table, but you are charged only for those you eat.

Rua da Mostardeira 4.
Tel: 266 707370.
http://otrovador.hi5.com.
Closed: Mon.

Restaurante Fialho ★★★★

A prize-winning, traditional restaurant located a little way from the centre but well worth seeking out.

Travessa dos Mascarenhas 16. Tel: 266 703079.
www.
restaurantefialho.com

ALMONDS

The pinky-white blossom of the almond trees in early February is one of the Algarve's most glorious sights, and an early sign that spring has arrived. The trees grow most abundantly in the Barrocal or limestone region of the Algarve, although, as agriculture has diversified recently, they have sadly become less common.

An old local legend has it that a northern princess married to an Arab king became homesick for the snowy lands of her birth. In order to ease her grief her husband secretly planted almond trees as far as the eye could see. The following February, she saw the trees thick with blossom, thought the ground was covered with snow and was instantly cured of her heartache. In fact, almonds probably existed in the province before the Muslim invasion. It is true, however, that the Arabs were the first to cultivate them, and the Arab word, almond (*amêndoa* in Portuguese), has remained in use to this day.

The Portuguese make good use of the nuts, which are harvested in August. In their simplest form, they are eaten as appetisers, roasted, fried or sprinkled with salt. They also appear on the Easter table in a thick coating of sugar along with the sugared white kernels of the *pinhão* (pine) nut – another Algarvian speciality – while the outer husks are traditionally burnt by potters in their kilns.

Various harsh-tasting liqueurs are distilled from the almond, of which *amêndoa amarga* is probably the best known.

Their greatest use, however, is in confectionery. There are few Algarvian sweets that do not include some form of almond paste. This is softer and sweeter than the marzipan of other countries, combining the almond with *ovos moles*, a gooey mixture of sugar syrup and egg yolks.

Marvão

O Sever ★★

Generous plates of locally raised pork and other meats, exceptionally well prepared; finish with a sampling of traditional sweets. Ask for advice on Alentejo wines to go with dinner.

Estrada do Rio Sever,

Portagem.
Tel: 245 993318.

Vila Viçosa

Os Cucos ★★

Large modern restaurant located in attractive wooded surroundings. Regional dishes.

Mata Municipal.
Tel: 268 980806.
www.cucos.web.pt

Wines of the Alentejo

Winemaking came to the Alentejo with the Romans, and has thrived and prospered for the 2,000 years since. Over the past two decades, however, there has been a major shift in production techniques, resulting in wines that are fast rising to the top ranks worldwide.

The wide rolling plains of the Alentejo scorch under blazing summer sun and shiver in the winter cold, extremes that combine with the region's varied soils to give the grapes the special qualities that make great wines. As the Alentejo wineries have invested heavily in the latest equipment and techniques for producing their wines, these factors have coalesced and the result is being hailed by connoisseurs worldwide.

Six different grapes, some of them peculiarly Portuguese, go into reds. Alfrocheiro, a grape used in the Dao region and believed to be Portuguese in origin, adds spice, the flavour of wild berries, and velvet textures. Aragonês is the Portuguese name for the Tempranillo grape, referring to its Spanish origins (it is known as Spain's 'Noble Grape'). Sometimes also called Tinta Roriz or Tinta Fina, it brings floral aromas with wood and peppery tones, along with fruit flavours of cherry, raspberry and redcurrant for deep, aromatic wines. Alicante Bouschet, a cross of the Grenache and Petit Bouschet grape varieties, brings a herbaceous quality and depth of colour. Castelāo, also known as Periguita, produces a hearty, robust wine noted for raspberry and spice flavours. Some link it to another grape, Trincadeira, grown mostly in the southern Alentejo and noted for its depth of flavour and capacity for ageing. Touriga Nacional, the grape used in northern Portugal to make Port wine, contributes intensity, ageing capacity and complexity. And in addition to these traditional and distinctly Portuguese grapes, Alentejo winegrowers have had considerable success with Syrah, often blended with Aragonês or Trincadeira.

While reds are king, Alentejo whites are also getting increased attention, especially after Tapada de Coelheiros Chardonnay 2003 won the Gold Medal as 'Chardonnay of the World'. Producers use Arinto grapes, also known as Pederña and a favourite in Vinhos Verdes, the light, slightly sparkling white wine produced in northern Portugal. This grape is valued for the hints of citrus it adds to wines. Antão Vaz is favoured for its complexity of tropical fruit flavours, and Roupeiro blends floral hints with tropical fruit.

Search out locally produced wines, found on every menu in the Alentejo. In tourist offices, ask for the booklet *Vinhos do Alentejo* and follow the 'Rota dos Vinhos do Alentejo' to visit wineries. Or sample several at the various wine producers' cooperatives. The region around Borba, near Estremoz, produces especially fine wines, which can be tasted at the Adega Coop. de Borba. Look especially for Adega Garrafeira and Cinquentenário, as well as any labelled 'Reserva'. Customised wine itineraries in the Alentejo and elsewhere in Portugal can be arranged by Cellar Tours (*www.cellartours.com*).

Alentejo vineyards

Accommodation

Several types of accommodation are available in Portugal, ranging from the luxurious pousada *to the smallest side-street* pensão. *If you have not booked in advance (necessary only in high season or in major resorts), it is worth checking out your options on arriving at your destination.*

In the unlikely event of finding all the official accommodation taken up, it is always worth enquiring about private rooms or flats for rent. Ask either at the tourist office or at a *pensão*.

Prices, no longer controlled by the state, vary enormously and will certainly be more expensive in the Algarve than the Alentejo. The tariff, listing the minimum and maximum charges according to the time of year, is attached to the back of each bedroom door. If you are travelling around with a friend, it is always cheaper to share a double room (*um duplo*) than for each of you to have a single room (*um quarto simples*). A room with a double bed is called *um quarto de casal*. Like most EU countries, when signing in at a hotel you will be required to submit your passport to the management for the purposes of official registration.

Pousadas

A *pousada*, which takes its name from the Portuguese verb *pousar*, meaning 'to rest', is a hotel owned by the state, although these are now operated by private hotel groups, which maintain the highest standards. The décor and cuisine reflect the customs of the area in which they are located. There are two types: regional *pousadas* are usually modern buildings situated in beautiful locations, such as the Pousada Santa Clara on the Alentejo/Algarve border; historic *pousadas* are converted buildings of historical significance, like the spectacular royal palace at Estremoz, now the Pousada da Rainha Santa Isabel. There are more than 40 *pousadas* throughout Portugal, with 12 in the Alentejo and 4 in the Algarve, but they are well distributed so that you can use them as bases for touring. Only a few have more than 20 rooms so it is wise to book well in advance.

Booking is through **Pousadas de Portugal**, whose website frequently offers promotions. Travellers over 55 who apply ahead get special discounts.

Rua Soares de Passos 3, Alto de Santo Amaro, 1300-314 Lisboa. Tel: 218 442001. Fax: 218 442085. www.pousadas.pt

Hotels

Portugal has five different grades of hotel, ranging from the de-luxe five-star category down to one-star. The grading is an official judgement of their quality and facilities. A five-star hotel will have a wide variety of services, ranging from top-quality food and sports facilities through to in-house entertainment and, in some cases, even private beaches. As the stars decrease, so do the amenities, but most hotel rooms down to two-star have an en-suite bathroom with bath. In all hotel categories, down to one-star, you will usually find that the accommodation is clean and the service efficient. Many hotels have a complaints book, but any serious inadequacies should be reported to the nearest tourist office. Service charges and taxes are nearly always included.

In the Algarve, self-catering hotels are especially popular. These often form

The de-luxe Hotel Alvor Praia, Alvor

The Hotel Penina Golf in Alvor

part of a large complex, with all the facilities of a conventional hotel, such as laundry and room-cleaning services, parking, telephone and television, but the guests are housed in a self-contained apartment or in a villa. They can be very cost-effective and are particularly good for families.

Pensions

In Portugal, a pension is called a *pensão* (plural: *pensões*). They are found in most towns and villages and they provide more modest accommodation than a hotel, though they, too, are graded and awarded up to three stars. Be aware that, like the hotel star ratings, these often relate more to the breadth of services than to the size or comfort of the rooms, so a two-star could have nicer rooms than a three-star.

It is always wise to inspect rooms and washing facilities before deciding to stay. Standards are usually good, however, and many *pensões* are as well equipped as a small hotel, while being considerably cheaper and often with a cosier and more friendly atmosphere. Some have restaurants but most only serve a fairly meagre breakfast of bread and coffee. A *residência* is similar in price and quality to a *pensão*, but an *albergaria* or *estalagem* is in the middle price bracket.

Country houses and manor houses

Visitors seeking the seclusion of the countryside, combined with the comfort of a fine, often traditional, Portuguese house, should investigate **Turismo de Habitação** (or **Turihab**). This scheme, supervised by the Portuguese tourism ministry, provides grants for owners of historically significant or beautifully located houses to create facilities for visitors.

There are three categories of property: Turismo de Habitação itself offers manor houses or architecturally distinguished buildings in which to stay; **Turismo Rural** provides properties usually in or near to country towns; while **Agroturismo** uses farmhouses or farm buildings and offers visitors the chance to be involved in the work of the farm. In general, the scheme provides an ideal way of getting to meet Portuguese people. Breakfast is provided and other meals can be requested. Booking is necessary and payment must be made in advance. Much more common in the north, a few of these are located in southern Portugal, most in the Alentejo. They are rated alphabetically, with an A rating being about the equivalent of a four-star hotel room. You should book directly with the owners or through the following associations:

Privetur (manor and country houses, farms and cottages).
www.privetur.co.uk
Turihab *Reservations can be made through its central booking office, CENTER (Central Nacional de Turismo no Espaço Rural). Tel: 258 931750. www.center.pt or by using the website www.solaresdeportugal.pt*

Youth hostels

There are around 40 youth hostels (*Pousadas de Juventude*) in Portugal, and the south has one of the best – at Alcoutim. In order to stay, you must have a valid International Youth Hostel Association card or obtain a guest card. Officially, you can only stay for three nights but this can be extended if space permits. The charge is nominal. For further information, contact the **Associação de Pousadas de Juventude** (*Rua Lúcio de Azevedo 27 1600-146 Lisboa. Tel: 217 232100. www.pousadasjuventude.pt. Email: informacoes@movijoven.pt*).

Camping

There are over 200 campsites in Portugal, many of them in outstanding locations and all at a very reasonable rate (*for further details, see* Camping, *pp178–9*).

The star ratings below are based on the approximate cost of a room for two people for one night in summer.

★ under €70
★★ €70–120
★★★ €120–175
★★★★ over €175

WESTERN ALGARVE
Albufeira
Hotel Montechoro ★★★★
The modern 360-bed hotel is set in garden-like grounds, only 1.5km (1 mile) from Praia da Oura and 3km (2 miles) from Albufeira centre. Attractive, comfortable rooms (all with balconies), adults' and children's pools, health club, eight tennis courts, squash and Turkish bath. Special rates available to guests for golf and horse riding.
Rua Alexandre O'Neill, 3km (2 miles) east of Albufeira.
Tel: 289 589423.
www.hotelmontechoro.pt

Aljezur
Carpe Vita ★
Newly built self-catering houses that sleep from two to five people are nicely furnished and equipped with kitchens or kitchenettes, located in the centre of old Aljezur.
Rua Serrado do Mosqueiro.
Tel: 963 256581.
www.carpe-vita.com

Carvoeiro
O Castelo ★★
A hospitable eight-room family-operated guesthouse with comfortable rooms, set on the cliff with balconies overlooking the town and beach. Comfort and convenience without stress.
Rua do Casino 59–61.
Tel: 282 083518.
www.ocastelo.net

Vale D'Oliveiras Quinta Resort & Spa ★★★
New to the Algarve, this five-star resort has 22 guest rooms, 2 suites and 80 one- and two-bedroom apartments, all with air conditioning. The apartments have a kitchenette and flat-screen TV with DVD player. Each dining room and terrace has views over the gardens and the village of Monchique. The resort has two tennis courts, two outdoor swimming pools, a heated indoor pool, bar, whirlpool, spa, sauna and gymnasium. The resort's Olive Tree restaurant serves light menus and gourmet cuisine, using ingredients from the resort's own organic farm.
Barranco Fundo, Apartado 79. Tel: 282 380560. www. valedoliveirasresort.com

Lagos
Hotel Solar de Mós ★★★
This family-operated 15-room hotel is only 1km ($^3/_4$ mile) from the beach. Beautifully appointed rooms come with an excellent breakfast. There are adults' and children's pools and kayak expeditions can be arranged.
Rua Santa Casa de Misericórdia 1, 3km (2 miles) west of Lagos.
Tel: 282 782579, 282 768301.
www.solar-de-mos.com

Portimão
Hotel Globo ★★
Modern city hotel. Rooms are clean and comfortable, and there

are good views from the restaurant and bar.
*Rua 5 de Outubro 26, 3km (2 miles) from Praia da Rocha.
Tel: 800 5281234.
www.hotelglobo-portimao. com*

Sagres
Martinhal Resort ★★★★
Opened in April 2010, this new high-luxury resort offers hotel accommodation in 38 rooms and suites as well as a wide range of ocean-view cottages and luxury villas. The five-star-rated resort has all of the amenities that one would expect, and even more. Its location at less congested Sagres is a plus, convenient for uncrowded beaches. O Terraço, its restaurant, quickly became a favourite for locals as well as hotel guests.
*Quinta do Martinhal, Apartado 54. Tel: 282 620022.
www.martinhal.com*
Memmo Baleeira Hotel ★★★★
Located at the very end of the main street in Sagres, the Memmo Baleeira has a stunning

setting on the cliff overlooking the fishing harbour and the lighthouse. Chic contemporary styling, a good restaurant, bar, pool, spa and Turkish bath add to the experience.
*Sitio da Baleeira.
Tel: 282 624212.
http://memmobaleeira. arteh-hotels.com*

Salema
Hotel Residential Salema ★★
Hotel Salema is located right on the beach in a fishing village. All rooms have balconies, most with a sea view. The very reasonable prices include breakfast.
*Rua 28 de Janeiro, Praia de Salema.
Tel: 282 695328.
www.hotelsalema.com*

EASTERN ALGARVE
Estói
Monte do Casal ★★★★
Located on the road between Estói and Moncarapacho, this beautifully converted and updated old manor-house inn is an island of peace and luxury. Daily

breakfast is served to guests on their own private balcony or terrace overlooking gardens, streams and pools. The service is warm and personal, and the dining room is superb. The spa is built among the pools with its own terrace.
*Cerro do Lobo.
Tel: 289 990140.
www.montedocasal.pt*
Poussada de Estói ★★★★
The guest rooms are in a new building, while the dining and common rooms are in the Palace of the Visconde de Estói. Opened in 2009, it is an outstanding experience, with gardens, pool, a good dining room and service to match. Only a few kilometres inland from the shore, this former palace is in the heart of the small town of Estói.
*Rua São José.
Tel: 289 990150.
www.pousadas.pt*

Faro
Hotel Faro ★★★
Guests at this four-star hotel in the heart of Faro have the best of both worlds: they can take the

hotel's free boat shuttle from the nearby marina to the beaches in the Parque Natural da Ria Formosa and return to choose from Faro's wide variety of restaurants in the evening.
Praça D. Francisco Gomes. Tel: 289 830830. www.hotelfaro.pt

Loulé
Loulé Jardim Hotel ★★★
Recently renovated, the rooms in this hotel are all air-conditioned and have LCD TVs. The in-town property has an internal garden, two bars and a private garage. The staff is happy to help arrange cycling, tennis, golf or other activities.
Praça Manuel de Arriaga. Tel: 289 413094/5, 968 691167. www. louléjardimhotel.com

Olhão
Pension Bicuar Residential ★
Clean, bright and attractive, this small lodging is in the centre of the old town. Views from its terrace are lovely. Guests enjoy free Wi-Fi and discount coupons

for breakfast at a neighbouring café.
Rua Vasco da Gama 5. Tel: 289 714816. www.pension-bicuar.com

Vilamoura
Crowne Plaza Vilamoura-Algarve ★★★★
This new beach and golf resort and conference centre is next to the casino and close to the beach and the Vilamoura Marina. It has 327 rooms with all of the expected amenities. The best golf courses in Vilamoura are only a few minutes from the hotel and Faro airport is 20 minutes away.
Rua do Oceano Atlantico Algarve. Tel: 289 381600. www.ichotelsgroup.com

LOWER ALENTEJO
Beja
Hotel Francis ★★
Comfortable hotel close to the Exhibition Fairgrounds, with bar, gym, Turkish bath and whirlpool. All rooms have air conditioning and TV.
Praça Fernando Lopes Graça. Tel: 284 315500. www.hotel-francis.com

Castro Verde
Aparthotel do Castro ★★
Simple but comfortable and attractive suites with kitchens, facing on to a central patio with a large swimming pool surrounded by orange trees. Free in-room Internet. Restaurants and attractions are within an easy walk and the staff is very helpful.
Rua da Seara Nova. Tel: 286 320250. www. aparthoteldocastro.com

Odemira
Casa da Seiceira ★★
Newly constructed, this small lodging has four rooms and three apartments attractively furnished in natural woods and bright colours. It is close to many Costa Vincentina beaches.
Chaminé 11, Brejão, São Teotónio. Tel: 965 064320. www.casadaseiceira.com

Serpa
Cantar do Grilo ★★
Nestled into the Alentejo countryside, this Swiss-owned hideaway provides four comfortable rooms and a

superb natural environment. It is known for its home-made country breakfasts.

Hardade Vale de Milhanos, Correio da Mó Apartado 668.
Tel: 284 595415, 961 043389.
www.cantardogrilo.com

Vila Nova de Milfontes
Pensão Eira da Pedra ★
Attractive lodging whose rooms offer the clean lines of minimalist furnishings, overlooking the dunes and beach, at rates from €30.
Rua das Pensões.
Tel: 283 998675.

Zambujeira do Mar
Monte do Papa Léguas ★★
Comfortable country atmosphere in an old farm ideal to get away from it all. Only 1.5km (1 mile) from the cliffs and beaches of Zambujiera, it offers cane-ceilinged rooms and three studios that cost only slightly more than the rooms. Farm-fresh eggs at breakfast.
Tel: 933 703724. www. montedopapaleguas.com

UPPER ALENTEJO
Elvas
Hotel São João de Deus ★★★
Close to the aqueduct, the hotel occupies an old convent. Its rooms are spacious and elegant and its Restaurante Dom Sebastião is highly regarded.
Largo São João de Deus 1.
Tel: 268 639220.
www.hotelsaojoaodeus.net

Estremoz
Casa do Terreiro do Poço ★★/★★★
In the heart of the fine wine area of Borba, this 30-room lodging is an oasis of beauty and calm. Elegant rooms open to gardens and a pool. Outstanding breakfasts are served in the pool pavilion in good weather. Several good restaurants are within a short stroll.
Largo dos Combatientes do Grande Guerra 12, Borba.
Tel: 268 808039, 917 256077. www.center.pt

Évora
M'ar de Ar Aqueduto ★★★★
The Aqueduto is a new hotel magnificently fitted into two historic structures just inside the walls of the old town. Strikingly modern, the spacious rooms are beautifully decorated. Many have balconies overlooking the aqueduct or the old town. The central gardens have a large swimming pool and sun terrace. The lounge and dining room of the Degust'AR Restaurant are fine examples of contemporary design. Friendly and attentive staff, valet parking and within walking distance of all the sights.
Rua Candido dos Reis.
Tel: 277 740700.
http://mardearaqueduto.
arteh-hotels.com

Marvão
Casa Dom Dinis ★★
Extremely well located in the centre of town, this is a small *pensão* with air conditioning and attractive, homely rooms. Views of Spain from their terrace.
Rua Dr Matos Magalhães 7.
Tel: 245 993957.
www.casaddinis.pa-net.pt

Practical guide

Arriving

Passports

Visitors from EU and Schengen zone countries can enter Portugal with either a valid passport or an identity card. Citizens from Canada, the USA, Australia and New Zealand must have a valid passport but don't need a visa unless they are staying for longer than 90 days.

By air

Southern Portugal has two major airports. The one at Lisbon (10mins from the city centre) would be the appropriate starting-off point for visiting the Alentejo, whereas Faro airport (about 15 minutes from town) would be suitable for visitors to the Algarve and the Baixo (Lower) Alentejo. Both are well equipped with post offices, shops, bars, restaurants and car rental facilities. Both are linked to their respective cities by regular bus and taxi services.

The Algarve can be reached via several budget airlines, including: **Jet2** (*www.jet2.com*), **easyJet** (*www.easyjet.com*), **Thomsonfly** (*www.thomsonfly.com*), **Monarch Airlines** (*www.flymonarch.com*) and **Thomas Cook** (*www.flythomascook.com*).

By boat

Brittany Ferries in England (*www.brittany-ferries.co.uk*) operates car ferry services between the British port of Plymouth and Santander in northern Spain. The sea journey takes approximately 20 hours and operates twice a week during the summer. The drive from Santander to southern Portugal is just over 1,000km (620 miles).

By road

Driving to southern Portugal can involve a long and exhausting journey (it is over 2,000km/1,250 miles from one of the French Channel ports to Lisbon, for example) and you may find it cheaper to fly to Portugal and hire a car on arrival.

By train

There is a train service available daily from London (Victoria) to Lisbon (Santa Apolonia) via Paris and Irun in northern Spain. The journey takes about 24 hours and involves changing trains (and stations) in Paris.

The *Thomas Cook European Rail Timetable* has details of train services, and is available to buy online at *www.thomascookpublishing.com*, from Thomas Cook branches in the UK or *tel: 01733 416477*.

Camping

Camping is a good option in Portugal since it is cheap and the 200 or so campsites are well kept and well situated. Sites are graded from one to four stars by the Ministry of Tourism and details are available from tourist offices or online at *www.roteiro-campista.pt*. Some of the campsites are large enough to accommodate up to 5,000 people and have furnished chalets available for rent, as well as shops and sports facilities. Passports must be left for the duration of your visit.

Camping away from official sites is not really approved of and is forbidden on beaches, in urban areas and within 1km (^{2}/$_3$ mile) of a campsite. For further details, contact **Federação de Campismo e Montanhismo de Portugal** (*Avenida Coronel Eduardo Galhardo 24D, 1199-007 Lisboa. Tel: 218 126890. www.fcmportugal.com*).

Children

The Portuguese are demonstratively affectionate with their own children and quite enthusiastic about other people's. Made-for-kids amusement and water parks are more common in the Algarve than in the Alentejo, but nearly every town has at least one well-equipped public playground. Several hotels provide specific entertainment for children and some also offer babysitting.

Supermarkets sell all the necessities, including disposable nappies, for baby care, but remember that supermarkets will be harder to find in the depths of the country. The only real danger to children's health is intense sunlight, so avoid prolonged exposure to the sun, and use plenty of high-factor sunblock.

Climate

Portugal is a temperate country but very sunny, especially in the south. June, July and August are the hottest months of the year with the temperature rising as high as 30°C (86°F) in the Algarve, higher in the Alentejo. Along the coast expect cool breezes in the evenings.

Spring starts as early as February. April and May are the best months to witness the splendid array of wild flowers. Summer is prolonged and it is still warm in late September. In recent years, October has been characterised by heavy rainfall in the south.

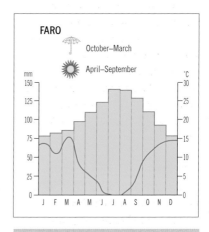

FARO

WEATHER CONVERSION CHART

25.4mm = 1 inch
°F = 1.8 × °C + 32

Conversion tables

See p180.

CONVERSION TABLE

FROM	TO	MULTIPLY BY
Inches	Centimetres	2.54
Feet	Metres	0.3048
Yards	Metres	0.9144
Miles	Kilometres	1.6090
Acres	Hectares	0.4047
Gallons	Litres	4.5460
Ounces	Grams	28.35
Pounds	Grams	453.6
Pounds	Kilograms	0.4536
Tons	Tonnes	1.0160

To convert back, for example from centimetres to inches, divide by the number in the third column.

MEN'S SUITS

UK	36	38	40	42	44	46	48
Portugal and rest of Europe	46	48	50	52	54	56	58
USA	36	38	40	42	44	46	48

DRESS SIZES

UK	8	10	12	14	16	18
France	36	38	40	42	44	46
Italy	38	40	42	44	46	48
Portugal and rest of Europe	34	36	38	40	42	44
USA	6	8	10	12	14	16

MEN'S SHIRTS

UK	14	14.5	15	15.5	16	16.5	17
Portugal and rest of Europe	36	37	38	39/40	41	42	43
USA	14	14.5	15	15.5	16	16.5	17

MEN'S SHOES

UK	7	7.5	8.5	9.5	10.5	11
Portugal and rest of Europe	41	42	43	44	45	46
USA	8	8.5	9.5	10.5	11.5	12

WOMEN'S SHOES

UK	4.5	5	5.5	6	6.5	7
Portugal and rest of Europe	38	38	39	39	40	41
USA	6	6.5	7	7.5	8	8.5

Clothes and shoe sizes in Portugal follow the standard sizes used in the rest of Europe.

Crime

Petty crime has increased greatly in recent years but it is still not a serious problem compared with many tourist destinations. Be on your guard against pickpockets in crowded places; and never leave anything of value in your car, wherever you park it. Never leave valuable possessions unattended on a beach. In hotels, it is usually possible to leave valuables in the hotel safe. Crimes should be reported to the local police within 24 hours.

Customs regulations

Visitors to Portugal may bring in clothing and other objects, such as a camera or a bicycle, as long as it is for personal use only. The same applies to small quantities of food with the exception of meat. Non-EU visitors may bring in up to 2 litres of wine, 1 litre of spirits and 200 cigarettes. There is no limit to the amount of currency that can be brought into the country, but sums exceeding the equivalent of €14,500 in foreign currency must be declared on arrival. When leaving, you may take out foreign currency up to the amount imported and declared. Domestic animals may only be brought into the country if accompanied by medical documentation to show that they are free from all serious diseases such as rabies and distemper. However, their return may be subject to quarantine.

Driving

To drive your own car in Portugal you must carry a valid driving licence and the vehicle registration documents. An international insurance certificate is compulsory. You should also carry a red warning triangle, and display it 30m (100ft) back from the rear of your car in the event of a breakdown or accident.

The Portuguese drive on the right-hand side of the road and use the international road sign system. Seat belts are compulsory and children under 12 cannot sit in the front seat unless strapped into a special child restraint.

Thanks to considerable new road building, motorways now connect Lisbon to the most heavily visited parts of the Algarve, and several towns that were bottlenecks along the coastal N125 have been bypassed. Mountain roads tend to be narrow and filled with hairpin turns, but the road surfaces are nearly always excellent. Bear in mind that in the country and in beach areas the roadsides may have a number of pedestrians. It is common to find flocks of sheep or other livestock crossing a road. Be aware that the legal blood alcohol limit is 0.05 per cent, and that drink-driving is being taken very seriously. Also be aware that others may not be so wary, and be cautious of often reckless drivers, who may be sober or not.

Petrol service stations are sparse in some inland regions, but plentiful on the N125, the Algarve's main east/west highway. The majority take credit cards. The N125 also has a number of orange SOS telephones in case of breakdown.

For more information, contact the **ACP (Automóvel Clube de Portugal)**, *tel: 808 502 502*, which has a reciprocal arrangement with other motoring associations, such as the British AA and RAC. It has a branch office in Faro and breakdown garages in Lagos and Portimão (*open: daily 8am–12.30pm & 2–6pm*).

Electricity

The current throughout southern Portugal is 220 volts AC and sockets accommodate the circular two-pin continental-style plug.

Embassies and consulates

Australia *Avenida da Liberdade 198, 2e, 1250 Lisbon. Tel: 213 101500.*
Canada *Avenida da Liberdade 198–200, 3rd Floor, 1200 Lisbon. Tel: 213 164600.*
Ireland *(consulate) Rua da Impresa 1, 4th Floor, Lisbon. Tel: 213 929440.*
UK *(embassy) 35–37 Rua de São Bernardo 33, 1249-082 Lisbon. Tel: 213 924000; (consulate) Largo Francisco A Mauricio 7, 1st Floor, Portimão. Tel: 282 490750.*
USA *(embassy) Avenida Forças Armadas 16, 1600 Lisbon. Tel: 217 273300.*

The old quarter of Vilamoura

The most common complaints are stomach upsets caused by a sudden change of diet and over-exposure to the sun. Break yourself in gradually to sunbathing and always use suntan oils or lotions.

Ask at your hotel or at a tourist office if you need a doctor or a dentist. At the chemist (*farmácia*), there are fully qualified staff who can deal with all minor ailments. If the chemist is closed, there will be a list on the door telling you where to find the nearest one that is open.

Emergency telephone numbers
All emergency services *112*.
Hospitals Faro (*tel: 289 891100*); Lagos (*tel: 282 770100*); Portimão (*tel: 282 450300*).

Health
No vaccinations are needed for a visit to Portugal. Under an EU reciprocal arrangement, visitors from EU countries are entitled to medical treatment in Portugal, but should obtain a free European Health Insurance Card from *www.ehic.org.uk*, by phoning *0845 606 2030* or from post offices. This should be presented to the doctor if possible before treatment or a consultation starts. Medical insurance is still advisable. Remember to keep all your receipts for making a claim.

Hitchhiking
Hitchhiking is legal but quite difficult from major towns. Country people are often friendly and responsive but seldom travel very far. Women travelling alone should avoid hitching.

Laundry
If you are staying in a hotel, it is likely to provide a laundry service. There are very few self-service launderettes in Portugal but there are many small laundries (*lavanderias*), while some grocery stores, and even small post offices, sometimes offer a service. Your clothes will come back immaculately cleaned and ironed, but be warned: Portuguese soap powders are often strong and may reduce the life of your clothes.

Lost property
Most towns have a lost-property office whose whereabouts can be obtained from tourist information centres.

Maps

Many new roads have been built in southern Portugal in recent years so maps can become out of date very rapidly. Michelin produces the best maps for Portugal and they are regularly revised. Town plans and local maps are usually available free from tourist offices.

Media

There are several newspapers and magazines written for the English-speaking visitor to the Algarve. *Get Real Newspaper*, published every Tuesday, is free in most supermarkets. *The Resident*, published every Friday, is available at newsstands, hotels and some expat bars. *The Portugal News* is the largest English-language newspaper, available throughout southern Portugal. There is also the glossy bi-monthly *Essential Algarve*. Tourist offices, and even hotels, sometimes produce news-sheets about forthcoming local events.

All the major international papers are available in the larger towns a day after their publication, but the *International Herald Tribune* normally arrives on the day it is printed.

Money matters

Portugal joined 12 other European countries on 1 January 2002 in exchanging its national currency (*escudo*) for the euro. Euro (€) note denominations are 500, 200, 100, 50, 20, 10 and 5. Coins are €1 and €2, and 1, 2, 5, 10, 20 and 50 cêntimos.

Banks are open Monday to Friday from 8.30am to 3pm. A commission is charged for changing money and it is advisable to take your passport with you. Many of the larger hotels will also change money but at a poor rate. Withdrawing from a home account with a debit card at an ATM gives the best exchange rate and is the most convenient, since they are available when banks are closed.

National holidays

1 January New Year's Day
February/March Shrove Tuesday
March/April Good Friday
25 April Liberation Day
1 May Labour Day
30 May Feast of Corpus Christi
10 June Portugal Day
15 August Assumption of the Virgin
5 October Republic Day
1 November All Saints' Day
1 December Restoration (of Independence) Day
8 December Immaculate Conception
25 December Christmas Day

Opening hours

Most shops are open weekdays 9am or 10am–1pm and 3–6pm or 7pm, and Saturday 9am–1pm. Shopping malls are open 10am–10pm or even as late as midnight. Saturday morning is the busiest and most popular time for shopping. National museums and galleries are open Wednesday to Sunday 10am–6pm, Tuesday 2–6pm, but are closed on Mondays. Some museums

Language

Portuguese is a Romance language (derived from Latin), so that you will find some written words familiar if you already have a knowledge of Italian, Spanish or French. On the other hand, the nasal pronunciation and the rapidity with which it is spoken can make comprehension quite difficult. Many Portuguese speak English, but your attempts to master a few phrases will be appreciated.

PRONUNCIATION

Words ending in the letter m sound like a combination of n and m so that *sim* (yes) should be pronounced seeng (but without really sounding the g). When the tilde accent (˜) appears over the letters ao, as in *não* (no), it sounds like a nasal ow with a hint of an oo sound following. The same accent over ae, as in *mãe* (mother), sounds like the y of my.

The consonants lh when combined, as in *talha* (butcher), sound like the ll in million. The combination of nh, as in *banho* (bath), is like ny in canyon. The j of *queijo* (cheese) sounds like the s of pleasure. The letter s before a consonant, or at the end of a word, should sound like the s of sugar; thus *Lisboa* (Lisbon) is pronounced Leeshboa.

NUMBERS

1	um (m)	16	dezasseis
2	dois (m)	17	dezassete
3	três	18	dezoito
4	quatro	19	dezanove
5	cinco	20	vinte
6	seis	21	vinte e um
7	sete	30	trinta
8	oito	40	quarenta
9	nove	50	cinqüenta
10	dez	60	sessenta
11	onze	70	setenta
12	doze	80	oitenta
13	treze	90	noventa
14	catorze	100	cem
15	quinze		

DAYS OF THE WEEK

Sunday	domingo
Monday	segunda-feira
Tuesday	terça-feira
Wednesday	quarta-feira
Thursday	quinta-feira
Friday	sexta-feira
Saturday	sábado

USEFUL WORDS AND PHRASES

yes/no	sim/não
hello	olá
good morning	bom dia
good afternoon/night	boa tarde/noite
goodbye	adeus
please	por favor
thank you	obrigada (f)
	obrigado (m)
you're welcome	de nada
today	hoje

tomorrow	amanhã	bathroom/toilet	casa de banho
yesterday	ontem	ticket/s	bilhete/s
I am English	sou Inglês	stamp/s	selo/s
do you speak English?	fala Inglês?	railway station	estação de comboios
how are you?	como está?	bus station	estação de camionetas
what is your name?	como se chama?	church	igreja
my name is...	chamo-me...	what do you call this in Portuguese?	como se diz isto em Portugues?
very well/good	muito bem/bom	please write it down	escreva-mo, por favor
see you later	até logo		
where is...?	onde é...?	what time is it?	que horas são?
what/when	que/quando	please!	faz favor
why/how	porquê/como	a table	uma mesa
how much is...?	quanto é...?	menu	ementa/lista
is there?/there is...	há?/há...	breakfast	pequeno almoço
near/far	perto/longe	lunch	almoço
here/there	aqui/ali	dinner	jantar
is there a pension near here?	há uma pensão aqui perto?	knife	faca
old/new	velho/novo	fork	garfo
cheap/expensive	barato/caro	spoon	colher
open/closed	aberto/fechado	glass	copo
right/left	direita/esquerda	starters	acepipes
for/to	para	soups	sopas
sorry	desculpe	first course	entradas
excuse me	com licença	desserts	sobremesas
I don't understand	não compreendo	dish of the day	prato do dia
I would like...	queria...	salt	sal
large/small	grande/pequeno	pepper	pimenta
more/less	mais/menos	to drink	para beber
do you have...?	tem...?	beer	cerveja
vacant rooms	quartos vagos	red/white wine	vinho tinto/branco
for two people	para duas pessoas	coffee	café
for one night/ week	para uma noite/ semana	milk	leite
do you know...?	sabe...?	the bill	a conta
could you...?	pode...?	braised	estufado/a
the key	a chave		

close for lunch. If you find a church or castle closed then go to the nearest bar or shop where you can usually track down the person responsible for the key.

Pharmacies
See Health, *p182*.

Places of worship
St Vincent's Anglican Church organises Sunday services at a number of places in the Algarve. For details, telephone the following:
Western towns *282 639774*
Central towns *282 338553*
Eastern towns *289 413564*

Roman Catholic services are held in English at **St Andrews Penina** (*tel: 282 459151*) and at Santa Maria church, Lagos, and at Fortaleza de Santa Catarina in Praia da Rocha.

The International Christian Fellowship meets each Sunday at 11am in the **Evangelical Baptist Church** (*Avenida 25 de Abril, Portimão. Tel: 282 461985*).

The International Community Church (Baptist) meets every Sunday at 10am (*Vila Praia da Dona Ana, near the Hotel Gofino, outside of Lagos. Tel: 282 086804*). There is also children's Sunday School.

Police
The police are quite numerous in towns and are generally helpful. They wear dark blue uniforms (brown in the country) and are responsible for public order and for traffic control. A red

A typical Alentejan church

armband indicates an ability to speak another language.

Postal services
You will find at least one post office (*correio*) in each town and a few exist in villages. They are open weekdays 9am–6pm and some on Saturday 9am–1pm, but smaller branches tend to close for lunch and on Saturday. Stamps (*selos*) can also be bought in shops displaying a *correios* sign. Poste restante mail can be sent to any post office in the country. It must bear the recipient's name, the address of the post office, and be marked *Lista de Correios*.

Public transport
Air
The national Portuguese airline, Air Portugal (TAP), connects Lisbon, Oporto and Faro.

Buses

Bus services, which link up most towns and villages, are run by a number of private companies. Fares are cheap but services can be slow. The main Algarve bus company is **EVA Transportes** (*www.eva-bus.com*). Timetables are posted at local bus stations or are available from tourist offices.

Bus stops are marked *paragem*; buses will not stop unless you extend your arm.

Trains

Train services are operated by **CP (Comboios de Portugal)**, the national railway network (*tel: 808 208208, from abroad: +351 213 185990. www.cp.pt*). A service runs from Lagos in the western Algarve to the eastern border at Vila Real de Santo António, with 50 stations in between. Several trains run daily and reservations are not necessary. Rapid Alfa Pendular trains link the Algarve with Lisbon (2hrs 45mins from Albufeira, 3hrs 15mins from Faro).

A street sign in Albufeira decorated with *azulejos*

Tickets for this service must be booked in advance. Timetables and booking are available online.

Senior citizens

Senior citizens get a discount of up to 50 per cent when travelling on the Portuguese Railway (CP). Low-cost flight-only deals are available, and it is often possible to rent a villa or apartment for an extended winter stay for a fraction of the high season price. Hotels, too, offer extremely attractive rates to elderly people staying for several weeks at a time. Many museums offer substantial discounts to the over 65s.

Student and youth travel

There are various schemes that enable young people to travel at a discount. An InterRail card allows people under 26 unlimited second-class rail travel throughout most of Europe and Morocco for one month.

Eurail is a similar, slightly more expensive, scheme for non-Europeans. In Portugal, it is possible to obtain reduced train fares by travelling in off-peak periods. Further details can be obtained from the information desk of Santa Apolonia station, Lisbon (*tel: 218 884025*).

Holders of an International Student Card, International Youth Card or an International Teachers' Card are entitled to a variety of discounts including travel and museum entry. Cards can be obtained from Youth

Travel Agencies. An International Youth Hostel Card will allow access to 41 hostels in Portugal. In the south, there are hostels in the Alentejo at Portalegre and in the Algarve at Alcoutim, Faro, Portimão and Lagos (*see p173*).

Sustainable tourism

Thomas Cook is a strong advocate of ethical and fairly traded tourism and believes that the travel experience should be as good for the places visited as it is for the people who visit them. That's why we firmly support The Travel Foundation, a charity that develops solutions to help improve and protect holiday destinations, their environment, traditions and culture. To find out what you can do to make a positive difference to the places you travel to and the people who live there, please visit *www.makeholidaysgreener.org.uk*

Telephones

It is important to realise that what appear to be area codes are a permanent part of the number and must be dialled even if you are in the place itself.

Public kiosks take phonecards which are available from post offices, shops and newsagents. If you use a phone in a hotel or a bar, be prepared to pay a surcharge.

For international calls, dial *00* followed by the country code, the area code (minus the initial *0*) then the number. Australia *61*, Canada and the USA *1*, Ireland *353* and the UK *44*.

Mobile access is quite good throughout southern Portugal, except in the more remote and mountain areas. Mobiles work on the GSM European standard, so UK, New Zealand and Australian mobiles work in Portugal; US and Canadian mobiles do not.

Time

Portugal observes Greenwich Mean Time in the winter (from the last Sunday in September to the last Sunday in March). Clocks then go forward by one hour for the summer, so except for a week or so in spring and autumn (to account for the different switch-over dates), Portugal is five hours ahead of Eastern Standard or Eastern Daylight Savings Time, and eight hours ahead of Pacific Time. South Africa is ahead by two hours, Australia by nine hours, and New Zealand by twelve.

Tipping

Most hotel and restaurant bills include a service charge; a small tip (10 per cent) for a meal, taxi or for hotel staff who have helped you will be appreciated, but is not essential.

Toilets

Public toilets are not common, except at railway stations and main bus stations. The facilities of a bar or restaurant can be used whether you are a customer or not. Facilities in the country may be a little primitive so it is well to take your own toilet tissue. Doors are usually marked *Homens*

(Men) and *Senhoras* (Women), but they usually have a pictorial symbol to aid the uncertain.

Tourist information

Every main town in Portugal has a local tourist office (or 'Turismo') which serves as an indispensable source of detailed information about local events and facilities. Not only will it provide you with free maps and leaflets (including timetables) but it will also give you a list of accommodation and restaurants. Nearly all tourist offices have an English-speaking member of staff.

The main office in the Algarve is at Faro: **Região de Turismo do Algarve**, *Rua da Misericórdia 8. Tel: 289 803604.*

Other main offices are:

Albufeira *Rua 5 de Outubro.*
Tel: 289 585279.
Évora *Praça do Giraldo.*
Tel: 266 777071.
Lagos *Rua Vasco da Gama (São João).*
Tel: 282 763031.
Loulé *Avenida 25 Abril 9.*
Tel: 289 463900.
Portimão *Avenida Zeca Afonso.*
Tel: 282 470732.
Tourist helpline (within Portugal)
Tel: 808 781212.

Travellers with disabilities

Both TAP Portugal and British Airways have facilities for travellers with disabilities such as wheelchairs at airports and transfer chairs. If you are taking a budget or charter flight, you should check with your travel agent whether comparable facilities are available. The Portuguese Railway (CP) has carriages with toilets adapted for wheelchair use and it gives priority to wheelchair users in the reservation of carriages. Large towns have some marked parking places for drivers with disabilities and these can be used by foreigners if their car is suitably marked. Tourist buses (Carris and Frota Azul Barraqueiro) can be hired which have facilities for people with disabilities.

Wheelchair hire can be found in most towns at Centros de Enfermagem (Nursing Centres). Consult your nearest tourist office or the reception of your hotel for the nearest one.

Wheeling Around the Algarve (*Rua Casa do Povo 1, Apartado 3421, 8135-905 Almancil. Tel: 289 393636*) is a specialist organisation that will arrange villa or apartment accommodation, transport, equipment rental, day trips and sport and leisure activities.

For further information and advice in the UK, contact the **Royal Association for Disability and Rehabilitation** (RADAR), *12 City Forum, 250 City Road, London EC1V 8AF. Tel: (020) 7250 3222. www.radar.org.uk*

The following is a selection of hotels with easy wheelchair access.
Albufeira Hotel Montechoro, Hotel da Aldeia.
Faro Hotel de Faro.
Lagos Hotel Golfinho, Hotel Meia Praia.
Monte Gordo Hotel Alcazar.

Index

Acknowledgements

Thomas Cook Publishing wishes to thank the photographers, picture libraries and other organisations, to whom the copyright belongs, for the photographs in this book.

ADEGA COOPERATIVE DE BORBA 169
ALLSPORT 152, 154, 156, 157
ANAL SHAH 9
BIGSTOCKPHOTO 16
DREAMSTIME 144
GETTY IMAGES 46, 121
OTTO PFISTER 74, 88, 130;
STILLMAN ROGERS 1, 22, 30, 38, 71, 76, 80, 81, 87, 91, 98, 113, 114, 119, 123, 125, 133, 140, 143, 149, 153
SPECTRUM COLOUR LIBRARY 17, 107, 129, 145, 163
THAKUR DALIP SINGH 89
THOMAS COOK 13, 23, 27, 47, 55, 61, 67, 97, 147, 155
WORLD PICTURES 120

The remaining pictures are held in the AA PHOTO LIBRARY and were taken by Jerry Edmanson, with the exception of pages 21, 45, 78, 128, 131, 166, 171, 172, 187, which were taken by Malcolm Birkitt, and page 161, which was taken by Wyn Voysey.

For CAMBRIDGE PUBLISHING MANAGEMENT LIMITED:
Project editor: Diane Teillol
Typesetter: Paul Queripel
Proofreaders: Kelly Walker & Jan McCann
Indexer: Marie Lorimer

SEND YOUR THOUGHTS TO
BOOKS@THOMASCOOK.COM

We're committed to providing the very best up-to-date information in our travel guides and constantly strive to make them as useful as they can be. You can help us to improve future editions by letting us have your feedback. If you've made a wonderful discovery on your travels that we don't already feature, if you'd like to inform us about recent changes to anything that we do include, or if you simply want to let us know your thoughts about this guidebook and how we can make it even better – we'd love to hear from you.

Send us ideas, discoveries and recommendations today and then look out for your valuable input in the next edition of this title.

Emails to the above address, or letters to the traveller guides Series Editor, Thomas Cook Publishing, PO Box 227, Coningsby Road, Peterborough PE3 8SB, UK.

Please don't forget to let us know which title your feedback refers to!